Testimonials: 'The Spiritual Route to Entrepreneurial Success'

John reaches out to an emerging group of entrepreneurs who seek a more enriching means of creating success. He defines a new paradigm of business that pursues purpose and passion, and demonstrates that one's own spirituality can be fully realised through the business of entrepreneurship. Readers will be inspired by this new model and will be eager to apply its principles in their own business.

Claudia Roth, Co-founder of ConsciousLab, a platform to raise consciousness in business

Compared to other books on Spirituality this one is unique. It deals with Spirituality within the world of business. In alignment with his own values John built, ran and sold a successful company serving clients across the globe. Using both inspirational and amusing anecdotes he demonstrates why trust wins out over control, co-creation beats coercion, integrity prevails over deceit and alignment with one's Higher Self creates win win solutions

Ian Patrick, Founder of the Course in Miracles Network in the UK, public speaker, frequent TV and radio guest and author of 'Of Course! How Many Light Bulbs Does It Take to Change?'

John Reynard is a man of our times. His journey as a leader and entrepreneur opened him up to a new paradigm of business and leadership that he brilliantly shares throughout this book. Join him in this journey to discover yourself as a visionary CEO shaping the future of Entrepreneurship in the 21st century.

Soleira Green, Founder of the Genius Company & the Visionary Network and author of 'The Real Art of Transformation'

THE SPIRITUAL ROUTE TO ENTREPRENEURIAL SUCCESS

From Harassed Sole Trader to Visionary CEO

JOHN REYNARD

authorHOUSE®

AuthorHouse™ UK
1663 Liberty Drive
Bloomington, IN 47403 USA
www.authorhouse.co.uk
Phone: 0800.197.4150

Published by AuthorHouse 04/06/2016

ISBN: 978-1-5049-9218-3 (sc)
ISBN: 978-1-5049-9219-0 (e)

To my father, who imparted to me a desire to shape
my own destiny and become an entrepreneur

CONTENTS

ACKNOWLEDGEMENTS

I would like to express my heartfelt gratitude to all those with whom I have come into contact in my business life. They include some of the most visionary and generous people you could ever wish to meet. Some of them are mentioned in the book, but for reasons of confidentiality where appropriate, I have changed their names.

I am eternally grateful to all those I have ever employed and had the pleasure of working with. They have taught me so much about myself, and I feel privileged to have had their dedication and commitment.

To my wife, Sue, who shares my interests in all matters spiritual. She has a creative flair for business and has stuck with me through thick and thin. On many occasions, she has brought a sense of practicality to my vague ideas and shown me another way of seeing whatever challenge was presenting itself. She also did a great job at proofreading this book.

To Sarah Alexander, who has given honest feedback on the message I have been trying to put across. In so doing, she has deepened my understanding of my own spirituality.

To Caroline Swain, who edited the book so thoroughly and in the process taught me how to write better English.

To Alison Goldie, who was the first to read the whole book and encouraged me to introduce examples from other successful businesses and to Alison McKenny, who took the photographs for the cover.

To Emile Kosviner, Ian Leppard, William Revell, Brian Courtney and Liam Mottram and all other friends and acquaintances, who have contributed insight, support and encouragement.

To those brilliant authors whose words I quote; they have provided huge inspiration to me.

To AuthorHouse, for publishing and presenting this book and bringing it to market.

FOREWORD

by Nick Williams

The interesting thing about John Reynard is that he has successfully integrated his sense of spirituality into his life as an entrepreneur. Although many view the world of business as unscrupulous and deceitful – the polar opposite of everything spiritual – he shows in this book how self-centred, egocentric thinking is actually counterproductive. Often with the use of amusing anecdotes, he demonstrates how trust, integrity, and compassion are essential to success and real abundance. I have read many books on how to succeed as an entrepreneur, but I do not know of any others written by someone who has lived out his spiritual principles and built a significant company.

John is not religious in the traditional sense – quite the opposite – but he does believe we all possess a Higher Self that is compassionate and loving, and that represents the truth of who we really are.

Those entrepreneurs who are constantly working in the business rather than on it, and who struggle to find the right staff, will be motivated to look first within themselves. They will see that blaming others and outer circumstances are easy options that in the end emasculate them. It will open their eyes to letting go of the barriers preventing them from attracting the right people. It will introduce them in a practical way to the benefits of staff participation in decision making and demonstrate how business can be taken to new heights once others are given freedom to express their own creativity.

Personally, I believe there are many in the business world who have similar beliefs to John but feel they cannot come out and say so. They fear they will be misunderstood, rebuked, and even mocked. This book will give them courage to be authentic in their own communications. Those entrepreneurs who do follow their gut instincts and know the value of so doing will recognise a lot of what John says about intuition. They will be delighted because he takes this whole subject to a much greater depth. For those with a definite spiritual interest, it will substantiate and explain a lot of what they have felt themselves but have never been able to put into words. It will inspire them and give them faith that living in alignment with their Higher Self, or Spirit, will lead them to success and abundance.

A key element of John's message is to follow one's inspiration – a subject close to my own heart. When I was a child, I felt I had a calling, something I was born to be and do. I was drawn to certain areas like literature and creativity, as if a natural intelligence was guiding me. But little by little I learned to mistrust and override that intelligence and do what I thought I was supposed to do. I listened and believed the voices of others rather than my own inner voice. I had a successful career in IT sales and marketing. On the surface I looked like a success, but I didn't really feel it. That voice of my natural intelligence was still there, nudging me to leave my corporate career behind, but I was too terrified to change.

I eventually had the courage to let go, and I started my own business. I have experienced many ups and downs, but twenty-five years later, I have written ten books, been invited to seventeen different countries to speak, and worked with many household companies. I feel I am fulfilling my own potential, and I believe this is what can happen for all of us when we follow our natural intelligence.

John is a passionate advocate of teaching entrepreneurial leaders to know that they have this deeper, natural intelligence. He is a flag bearer for a new generation of entrepreneurial leaders who are seeking entirely new ways of doing business. He helps them understand that by aligning with their Higher Selves, they will be guided to make wise and truly intelligent decisions that will help them create sustainable long-term business success.

The book outlines a clear journey of how it is possible to move from being a harassed sole trader to an enterprise that functions consistently and profitably without their daily involvement. It is a very readable book for open-minded entrepreneurs, and it describes the route to becoming a truly visionary CEO.

Read on, and be inspired.

Nick Williams
Author of *The Work We Were Born to Do* and *Unconditional Success*

WHO THIS BOOK IS FOR

This is not another book about best practice and how to succeed in business; there are plenty of those already. It is for those who have a passion for entrepreneurship, who seek to prosper, and who want to build their dreams in accordance with their highest thinking and beliefs.

Entrepreneurs bring about innovation and effect change. Without them, the economy would stagnate. We are all familiar with the likes of Sir Richard Branson and Lord Sugar, but for every entrepreneur who has made a million, there are thousands who struggle for years and only partially succeed. They work incredibly hard, take huge risks, create employment for others, sign over their homes to merciless banks, and pay their full share of taxes. All this, and yet they never attain the levels of return they truly deserve.

Such was my own case. I had turned sixty by the time I created a business that ran independently of me and generated sufficient profit to cover more than my living costs. I had some good years, but they were always interspersed with poor ones, and the latter quickly drained away any assets I had accumulated. Whilst those around me seemed to go from strength to strength, I felt stuck in the doldrums and very alone. I suspect many entrepreneurs empathise with this plight.

My own situation began to change when I ceased separating my spiritual life from my business life and committed to integrating the two. I had always reckoned there was more to life than a one-way ticket from cradle to grave. I have always thought that within each of us, there is an essence, a Higher Self that is pure, remains forever unblemished, and seeks the best for everyone. I believed this but failed to live out such spiritual principles in my day job. I was fearful that if I made reference to them, I would not be taken seriously and would even be ridiculed. I conformed, but whilst I thought I was playing safe by denying my spirituality, I was actually creating a split that was costing me my success. There was a rift between how I showed up in business and my real, authentic self. I was blocking access to my own essence, my core being, and the source of my spontaneity, creativity and power. I held myself back from abundance and confined myself to mediocrity.

A major theme of the book is that we create our own worlds. The state of our business reflects the state of our mind. When we genuinely feel positive and our head and heart are aligned, we attract positive results. When we are joined with our Higher Self, that essence within us that is all-knowing, we embark on an awesome journey that leads us to a deep sense of fulfilment. Every time we pursue negative thoughts, they get reflected back to us, usually in the form of problems. But there are no challenges without purpose; each and every one comes for a reason. By accepting, understanding, and healing our negative attitudes and beliefs, we transform them, grow as people, and attract real abundance into our lives.

This book will be of little interest to those arrogant enough to believe they have a Midas touch that turns everything into gold. Neither will it speak to those who have no belief in anything beyond what is immediately in front of them. It is for entrepreneurs who are open to looking at their lives differently and want to understand who they really are. It is a book about how to realise our full potential through self-empowerment, cooperation with others, and alignment with our Higher

Selves. It seeks to demonstrate that entrepreneurship provides a meaningful vehicle through which we can discover the lives we are truly destined to live. It will inspire:

- harassed sole traders and small company entrepreneurs who value integrity and want to grow their business to a size where it is no longer dependent on them and achieves significant inherent value
- entrepreneurs and forward-thinking company executives who seek to live their business lives in alignment with their highest ideals

CHAPTER 1

Personal Story

Initiation into Business

I have only ever been employed for three years, and that was at the beginning of my career. After reaching the end of my student days, I looked at my contemporaries taking up what seemed to me to be rather humdrum nine-to-five jobs, and I thought, 'This is not really what I want.' I knew it was time to earn a living, and I was ready to commit to a regular job, but there in the background lurked a niggle, a desire to add something a bit extra. I had lived in London and enjoyed it, but now I was keen to live abroad. I felt drawn to France. My view was that if I was going to settle into a job, I'd rather do it in a place where I could also experience a different culture and learn another language.

I had qualifications in market research and a basic level of French. I wrote to twenty research companies in Paris and offered myself up for employment. To my amazement, the CEO of a large multinational, happened to be in London two weeks later, and he invited me to meet with him for an hour. After I arrived at his hotel and announced myself, he greeted me cordially in French. Unfortunately, I was so nervous I struggled to string any French words together and he had to switch to English. I was convinced I had blown my chances, but at the end of the meeting, he did say that if I was serious I should go and see him in Paris. He didn't offer to pay my fare, and he certainly did not lead me to think highly of my prospects, but he left the door open.

A couple of months later, I decided to take the plunge and go. I was more coherent this time, albeit not outstanding. To my absolute amazement at the end of the interview he offered me a three-month trial. I was flabbergasted and immediately accepted. I had landed a job with a great company, a household name. My salary was to be one-third higher than what I was getting in the UK, and I was to move to a city I have loved ever since.

This showed me that when we listen to our instincts, formulate ambitious ideas and follow through, something many people call *luck* steps in and favours us. I was a good candidate but was not exceptional, and the CEO was not actively looking for a new recruit. Maybe he saw the usefulness of having a native English speaker on his team; maybe he liked and responded to the initiative I had demonstrated by making contact directly with him. I do not know. The end result was much better than I had ever anticipated.

During my first three months I was allocated a personal mentor and he took genuine interest in helping me settle in. He was in his late thirties, somewhat opinionated, and definitely outspoken. I could see how he upset higher management and did not fit the mould. Large multinationals can be great training grounds, but they have a dark side, and if you alienate yourself by consistently refusing to conform, you run the risk of becoming a casualty. My mentor certainly worked hard and was bold. He almost brought in a contract with a major car manufacturer that would have transformed the company. Had he succeeded, he would have been everyone's darling. Unfortunately, this was not the case, management decided he had to go – and the sooner, the better. He arrived at work one day to find his name published in the internal company magazine as having already left. The CEO was contrite; it was all a dreadful mistake. It had been agreed privately that my mentor had three months to find another job and that nothing would be said officially until then. Somehow, a 'mistake' in the editing of the magazine occurred, and his departure was prematurely announced. He emptied his desk and left immediately, feeling deeply embarrassed and abused. In his eyes he had been publically humiliated, and he was convinced the premature publishing of his name was deliberate.

The attitude to my mentor's challenging character and the suspicion around how he was dispatched showed me what I did not want to be part of. A large company's internal politics can be such a drain on everyone's energy, kill motivation and creativity, and ultimately damage the company itself. I was young and wanted to make a contribution, but I felt I could not express myself freely in such an environment. After three very enjoyable years, I felt that was enough. I sensed that were I to stay longer, I would be absorbed into the system and become dependent upon it. I resigned, took a long holiday, and turned to freelance market research. My intention was that in so doing, I would open myself up to something that truly inspired me.

First Enterprise

One great advantage of freelancing is you can do other things alongside your primary job. I had been left some money on the death of my mother, and it was enough to make a significant deposit on a property. I bought a two-hundred-year-old bakery with the intention of converting it to a vegetarian restaurant. I was vegetarian myself at the time and had a vision of creating a meeting place for like-minded people. I gathered friends, family, and anyone else I could muster to help with the conversion, and after a year we finally opened.

I enjoy marketing, so creating a buzz and getting folks into the restaurant came naturally to me. Our opening night was crazy. I was upfront waiting on customers, and I remember at one stage people were shouting out requests from so many different directions that I completely lost track and my mind went blank. The only thing I remember was realising I had to get out before anyone threw any more demands at me.

We did survive our grand, if somewhat unpolished, launch. We hastily improved the service and kept the place in the public eye by creating theme nights. We had belly dancers, calypso bands, and flamenco dancers. The atmosphere was lively and invigorating, and we always sold out on these occasions.

After a couple of years, I came to the realisation that I was not happy. I had been working seven days a week, and fatigue was getting to me. I used to wake up on Monday morning thinking, 'Thank goodness it's Sunday and I have a day off.' Then my heart would sink at the realisation it was actually Monday again. Although our theme nights were successful, there were many other nights when hardly anyone showed up; the business was variable and unpredictable. I felt trapped and could not see a solution. I had started the venture with no previous restaurant experience and had made all sorts of errors.

Above all, I lacked the maturity to create a good life balance. I worked too many hours, failed to take any breaks, and continuously worried about finances. Instead of keeping fresh, I allowed myself to get dragged down by minutiae. Whilst I was going about my daily tasks, my energy was scattered, and my mind constantly flipped from one thing to another. To most people I may have appeared fine, but I felt wretched inside, was constantly on edge, and worried that the business would fail. I often wonder how many other entrepreneurs go through such slumps.

I realise now I had lost connection with my inner core, that essence within all of us which is characterised by hope, that nucleus that can feel peace no matter what is going on externally – my Higher Self. During this time, a close friend, whom I suspect did see my distress, gave me the name of a Jungian psychotherapist. I had always been interested in personal growth, but at the same time I was suspicious and frightened of revealing my true feelings and my real self. However, desperate times called for desperate measures. I recognised I needed help, called the psychotherapist, and made an appointment. We clicked from the start. I felt a deep level of acceptance, and during the sessions I started to open up in ways I had never done to anyone else. In a matter of weeks, I became more centred and regained confidence. I was able to be honest with myself: the life of a restaurateur was not my cup of tea. I had enjoyed getting it off the ground, but I was no chef, and waiting on customers every day was not enough. I could have stepped to one side, remained as owner, and let others run it and pay me a rent, but it was too late for that. I needed a complete break.

I put the restaurant up for sale. Thanks to the inner work I had done I was able to be completely open with my staff. Within a month a buyer stepped forward and bought the whole enterprise exactly as it stood. Everyone who wanted to stay kept their jobs, and I returned to life as a freelance researcher.

Life as a Sole Trader

Most businesses start from a spark of an idea, an inspiration that comes with an uplifting feeling, with a definite and clear excitement. After the restaurant sale, I remember walking along the cliffs of South Devon, totally absorbed in the stunning beauty of the landscape. Suddenly and quite out of the blue, it became clear: I wanted to set up my own market research company. I had had enough of taking on projects defined by others. I wanted to be in charge. Freelance is great for variety and flexibility, and the income can be rewarding, but it no longer sufficed.

I started making calls, introducing myself to prospective companies and then going to visit them. It took six months to win my first job and get it commissioned. My focus was on business-to-business market research, and at one stage I extended the offering to include marketing consultancy to professional firms. I lived the life of many sole trader entrepreneurs: in the profitable times life was good, but in the poor years it was a struggle.

Transition to SME

In 2004 I married Sue. She had become my business partner after working with me for several years. Together we took a strategic decision to concentrate on market research within the niche sector of medical devices. Such products include blood glucose meters, asthma inhalers, and all the varied kit used in hospitals by anaesthetists and surgeons. We had complementary skills: she was a trained librarian with an eye for detail, and she had previously worked for a pharmaceutical company. My own training had been in market research, and I enjoyed the consultative sales approach.

We won some decent projects in our first years, but everything remained stop-start. I would go out and present our services. We would land a project, get totally involved in it for however long it took, and then find ourselves back at square one with the need to find more work. Ongoing continuous work eluded us.

One day we had a break. A new client had a product they had just launched, and they asked if we could monitor its acceptance and progress in the market, in particular their customers' reactions to it. We did a good job, and the project grew in size and was repeated twice a year. We now had a reliable stream of work – the essential core for any business – and life began to feel more stable.

An opportunity came up to buy a newly built office on the other side of the road from where we were operating, in a small rented property. Logically we did not need more space, but there was no way we could expand. I have heard it said that once all available space is full, there is a psychological barrier to growth; business plateaus, and there is unconscious resistance to further expansion. I now believe this is true. We bought the new office and shortly afterwards discovered we needed more help. Not only were we able to accommodate new people immediately, but we attracted higher calibre graduates because we looked more professional in our new environment.

Attracting the right staff and inspiring them to give their best is key to taking a two-to-three-person operation that pays an income to its owners to a full-blown business with its own intrinsic value. When a business thrives without the daily input from its proprietors, it stands a chance of being sold as a fully autonomous company, and that is a far more financially rewarding result than simply earning a living. In addition, all those involved in the business get to continue and evolve into the future, which is something they deserve.

Building a good team is the biggest barrier to success for many entrepreneurs. It was definitely a massive challenge for Sue and me and we made many mistakes. It seemed we just could not find decent staff who could do the job we wanted – or if we did, we managed them poorly and they left.

It was only when we started to realise that we were the source of our own problems that we began to see things differently. We understood that the people we were attracting into our lives were reflecting back to us where we were within ourselves. If we believed no one could do a job as well as we could, they proved themselves incapable. If deep down I did not want someone to be as good a salesperson as me, he or she was not. We were manifesting our own obstacles!

We asked ourselves what we were doing to attract the situations in which we found ourselves. If someone displayed a characteristic we did not like, we questioned ourselves as to what it was they were reflecting within ourselves. We sought professional help and became skilled at a technique called the

Clearing Process, which was devised and taught by Sandy Levey-Lunden and her colleague Len Satov. We actively applied this methodology to many different scenarios, and our expectations of others, and communications with them steadily improved. We grasped the benefits and joy of delegation of responsibility to others. We attracted team members who not only performed better than we could have imagined but shared our own core values of integrity, commitment, and respect for others. We gelled as a team, being at work was a real pleasure, and the business grew quickly as a result.

The Management Buyout

As our lives progress, our interests evolve. If we can recognise and go with such shifting energies, we retain our freshness, regardless of age. My trust in others had deepened. I could see that each time I delegated an aspect of my own role that had lost its thrill for me, the new person put their own creativity into it and took it to a new level. This was a truly liberating experience, and I was able to let go of more and more, including the daily management of the business. In the end I concentrated on sales to new clients, and ultimately I was happy to let this go too. I was now ready to move on to the next stage of my life.

We initiated a management buyout, or MBO. I liked the idea of the business being taken forward by those who had worked so closely with us and had done so much to build it. We already had someone in place who was keen to step up and take over. After a false start with a company that failed to understand our needs, we identified a capable firm of MBO specialists to guide us through the process. Their fees made my eyes water at first, and I doubt we would have entertained them had we not suffered the earlier aborted experience. As is so often the case, you pay for what you get. Our new advisers counselled us through many complex negotiations, and we signed a deal that we all understood and were happy with.

After years of the typical life of a sole trader entrepreneur, oscillating between feast and famine, success and struggle, my wife and I had started a new business that truly matched our skills and enthused us. We were assisted by a great team and built one of the fastest-growing market research companies in Europe. We experienced growth rates of 60 per cent per annum when lots of companies were cutting back due to recession, and our clients included eight of the top fifteen blue-chip multinationals in the healthcare sector. We negotiated an MBO in which all members of staff kept their jobs, and new posts were created. We came away from the business financially sound and with a real sense of achievement.

Work with Others

I am not religious and have no appetite for any form of dogma. On the other hand, I do believe that we all possess a Higher Self that is compassionate, generous, and loving. It is this Higher Self that is connected and aligned with Spirit; the essence within each of us, which is all-seeing and remains forever changeless. It is our Higher Self which represents the Truth of who we really are.

Most people see no connection between what is perceived as the ruthless world of business and all matters spiritual; in fact, they view them as diametrically opposed. Personally, I have always been excited by how our Truth can be expressed in every aspect of life, including entrepreneurship. Now that I have learned to apply spiritual principles to business, I have witnessed their value. I speak at those forums where people are interested to hear about how the use of intuition, meditation, trust, and alignment with our Higher Selves contributes to abundance and well-being. I love working with companies who put staff involvement and fulfilment high on their agenda, and I want to see them succeed.

For Your Consideration

Take a little time to reflect on your own situation. Make some notes for yourself. I know it's tempting to keep reading, but the book will provoke ideas, and it's important you do not lose them.

1. When in your business life has everything flowed relatively effortlessly and been totally enjoyable?

_____

_____

_____

_____

_____

_____

_____

_____

_____

_____

_____

_____

2. What made those times so good?

_____

_____

_____

_____

_____

_____

_____

_____

_____

_____

_____

_____

_____

_____

3. In what areas of your business do you feel you struggle
    and maybe even feel stuck?

_____

_____

_____

_____

_____

_____

_____

_____

_____

_____

_____

_____

_____

_____

_____

CHAPTER 2

The Power of Intuition

What Is Intuition?

Intuition enables us to see behind statistics and forecasts, make useful predictions in spite of incomplete information and take original decisions that bring about win-win solutions. Successful entrepreneurs recognise its potential and take heed of it.

Intuition is an inner voice that we all possess. It is an astute counsellor that nudges us forward in our lives. It comes with an uplifting feeling and is never manipulative. It is the voice of our Higher Selves and it unlocks creativity, makes life smoother, more fun, and sometimes defies logic, at least initially.

Intuition comes to us spontaneously, often as a feeling or even a voice. It is clearest when we are quiet and centred within ourselves, but it can also come to us during moments of extreme stress. It can be scary, especially at first, because it stretches us and takes us beyond our comfort zones. It is complementary to logic and is not a replacement. It always pays to understand the facts before applying our intuition and making important decisions.

In today's world, we have become excessively dependent on our analytical minds, and all too often we ignore our intuition. We grow up in families where we learn to override our instincts and do what is expected. Our inner spark is suffocated and we become disinterested and apathetic. Intuition can never be lost, however – quite the opposite. It can be fully activated at any age.

As with all skills, the more you tune in to your intuition, the better you get at recognising it and the more confident you become in following it. Ultimately, you notice that people pay more attention to you and pick up on your ideas. You enjoy being authentic, and although some may initially resist what you have to say, they usually come around over time.

The Importance of Intuition

Sue and I were once encouraged by a business adviser whom we very much respected to meet a firm of specialist tax consultants from a different part of the country. He believed they were offering something quite innovative, and it would be in our interests to hear what they had to say. We went to the meeting with an open mind. The two partners of the firm arrived, a lady and gentleman, and they convincingly presented their case. They put forward an attractive offer: by using their services, we would save significant amounts of tax. Our adviser stressed that he had already worked with this particular firm, and in his opinion, they were entirely reputable.

As a prerequisite to engaging them, we had to sign a non-disclosure agreement (NDA). The reason for this was that they had such a unique service that they wanted to ensure it remained confidential and would not be passed on to any of their competitors. However, there was one short paragraph in it that did not make sense. I pointed this out, and it was corrected, but I did wonder how such a crucial and presumably well-used document could contain such a flaw. Everything they said was entirely logical, and the offer was certainly enticing, but there was something in the lady's tone of voice that did not sit well with me. I could not fault anything she said, but intuitively I felt uneasy in her presence. Combined with the previous error in the NDA, I thought I would look into the matter further.

I knew other professionals in the part of the country where the tax consultants were based, and I called them to enquire whether they knew the lady. They certainly did – and they were very explicit about why we should not work with her under any circumstances. That was sufficient for me, and we discontinued the contact. Two years later, I heard that the firm had been dissolved. The lady had been exposed for conducting sharp practices and had disappeared, leaving all sorts of debris behind her. I dread to think of the chaos we would have got ourselves into had we engaged them. At minimum, we would have suffered a distressing and time-consuming tax investigation. Normally I would not have questioned the initial recommendation we received because it was from a trusted source, but my intuition guided me otherwise.

Our intuition knows so much more than we do, and it is always seeking to guide us. It adds another dimension to our decision making, and the more we cultivate and tune into it, the more helpful it is. Many poor decisions are based on appearances and partial facts, especially if there is an easy win involved. Whenever we face a decision with which we feel uncomfortable, we need to check in with our intuition and ask more questions until we are happy with what we are doing, find another way, or pull out.

How to Develop Intuition

When we consciously decide to recognise our intuition, it willingly and increasingly communicates to us; by allowing it space and giving it focus, we strengthen it. We nurture our intuition by regularly absorbing ourselves in activities that take us completely away from our routine thinking, out of our heads, and into our bodies. For me, this is through meditation. For others, it might be walking or running in nature, horse riding, or dancing to music. The main criterion is that it be pleasurable and regular; it is too easy to get busy and make excuses. It is when we get back to our true selves and feel relaxed and centred that we allow space for our intuition to come through.

Some people pick up intuitive messages through visual stimuli; others get them through smell or touch. These are not usual for me, but I'm sure they work for others. My own intuition works well when I have been dwelling on a problem, understand the situation as best I can, and have considered the various options. I then let the whole matter go and do something completely different, or if it's late, I go to sleep. Once I give myself a break and let my unconscious mind do the work, my intuition has the opportunity to make its contribution.

I also find that my intuition is active when I travel. When I'm on the move and put distance between myself and my daily life, I spontaneously receive insight. This happens so often that I always travel with a ready means of making notes. I also do whatever I can to make my journeys as stress-free as possible. When the situation is fraught, the mental chatter is deafening, and intuition is suffocated.

Intuition is also nurtured by the giving of thanks and the expression of appreciation. Every time we thank someone for what they have done, and each time we truly appreciate our surroundings and what we already have, we deepen our connection to our intuition.

It is certainly possible to remain connected to intuition when there's a lot going on, but it is important to keep breathing and to feel what is happening in the body. When we are harassed we go into our heads and our breathing becomes shallow. The way back to intuition is to slow down, become mindful, observe, and feel what is occurring internally.

Stress, overtiredness, poor diet, and lack of exercise dampen our intuition. If you have a habit of not taking a break at lunchtime, or you spend your day hunched over a computer, you risk losing touch.

Cost of Ignoring Intuition

The intuitive voice guiding us to stop doing something is clearer and more discernible than the one urging us to try something new. This is probably because the message 'stop' is simpler and easier to understand than one encouraging us to open up to something we have not yet considered – or so you might think.

My wife and I were on holiday in Turkey. Everything was going well, and we had got to know several people staying at the same residence. One afternoon we were sitting around the pool relaxing. I happened to hear a few of the others discussing the possibility of going paragliding. It was always something I had fancied doing, and so I joined the group.

The next day as we were driven to the offices of the paragliding company, we were joking around, and the anticipation and excitement were palpable. We encountered Hector, the guy in charge. His first words were, 'You need to hurry – we only have five minutes.' He was obviously irritated and in a bad mood, and we all felt uncomfortable. This was the first sign to me that maybe this was not going to be a good day.

A few minutes later, we got onto the company's minibus to take us to the top of the mountain. It was a fifty-minute journey up to a height of six thousand feet. Everyone else seemed to settle down, but I could not help but notice that our pilots, the young guys who would be flying us down, looked totally disinterested. They were slouched in their seats looking withdrawn, as though they couldn't care less. I supposed to them we were just another set of bodies to be transported. I really didn't like this, and I could hear my inner voice saying, 'Something is wrong here.'

We arrived at the mountain top and found chaos. Lots of others were already there rushing around; it looked like anarchy. Eventually I found my pilot, a grumpy lad with only a few words of English, and I suddenly realised I was entrusting my life with him. He fitted my gear on and attached himself behind me. He then briefly explained that I should hold onto this and that rope, but not touch another, and simultaneously run forward six to seven paces towards the cliff edge. By this time I felt very uncomfortable indeed. I realise now I could have insisted on more explanation or another pilot, or even pulled out. But in the heat of the moment, I overruled my intuition and continued.

We began our run to the cliff edge, and to my horror, after just three or four steps, I stumbled to the left and almost hit the ground. The MBT sandals I was wearing had a rocking sole – good for posture, but not for running. Fortunately, I managed to recover, sprung back up, and continued. We did take off, but my pilot was incensed because he had not realised I had stumbled. He thought I was trying to sit down too quickly into the supporting sling, an act which normally results in rapid descent over the cliff edge. Thank goodness we did get airborne, but I felt severe pain in my ankle and feared I had broken it. I began to worry about how I would cope with the landing, because I would again have to run several steps, but with much relief I survived. I kept my weight on my right foot. After some emergency treatment, my wife aided me, and we returned home with me on crutches. I was laid up in plaster and then fitted with an orthopaedic boot and incapacitated for four months. I could not work and was acutely restricted. Altogether it was an extremely tedious and disagreeable experience.

This incident really demonstrated to me how our intuition works. It starts by giving us gentle hints that we are involved in something inappropriate to our well-being. If we ignore such indicators, then it patiently reminds us again, even several times, but with increasing urgency and alarm. Eventually, if we continue to take no notice, we are brought to a dramatic halt and have to suffer the consequences. I could have pulled out after just two minutes with Hector, and I certainly could have demanded clearer instructions before take-off. Both would have been positive options. If I had stopped and observed that I had to run over rough ground, I might also have realised I was not wearing the correct footwear. Subconsciously, a part of me knew I was heading towards an accident, and my intuition was trying to tell me to extricate myself. I chose to ignore it and paid the price.

Breaking bones and painful accidents are extreme situations. On a daily basis, our intuition is available and can give us guidance in all manner of ways. We might for example be driving to an appointment and intuitively feel we should take one route rather than another. We follow our intuition and discover later that we avoided a nasty traffic jam.

Proactive Use of Intuition

As we become proficient at tuning into our intuition we can apply it pro-actively to complement our decision-making. Penny Peirce gives appropriate background in her book *The Intuitive Way*.

> The body's rapport with the natural environment, or Higher Guidance, comes from the collective consciousness of the planet. When something is right for us we experience feelings of positive expansion,

deep comfort, even heightened enthusiasm.
When something is wrong or inappropriate
we feel contracting energy, withdrawal and
our energy drops. We might even get a sense
of impending depression.

When seeking to use our intuition pro-actively it is important to take a couple of deep breaths, close your eyes, and step back from any immediate emotional ties to the issue. Your intuition is best at addressing questions that require a clear yes or no. Hence, you get the best results by formulating your question in such a way that a yes or a no will give clarity. You might be making an offer to purchase a particular product, for example, and the price is negotiable, but you suspect that somewhere between £500 and £2,000 is appropriate. Instead of asking, 'How much should I offer?' it works better to break out the possible answers and then ask separately for each option: 'Should I be asking £500? £1,000? £2,000?' Feel the energy associated with each response. The right answer will carry more vitality and enthusiasm.

The first answer to your question is usually the best one. Anything that comes later risks being influenced by your customary limiting beliefs. Your habitual patterns of thinking may fear the change to which your intuition wants to guide you: they can put up strong resistance in all sorts of subtle and clever ways. It can become challenging to tell the difference between what your intuition is saying and what your more narrow-minded voice of the past is making up.

With practice and experience, we become more and more proficient at recognising our intuitive voice. We will certainly make mistakes, but when we do, we will detect an increasing anxiety signal, and at that moment we need to reassess. Either we need to ask the question again but take more time over it and go deeper within ourselves, or we need to redefine the question in a clearer way.

On some occasions, we will get no answer at all. Although this is initially frustrating, it is immensely useful. It often indicates that the timing is wrong or the question is inappropriate, and that at least for the moment we need do nothing.

Another way of proactively asking for intuitive guidance is to invite it to come during sleep. As you lay your head on the pillow, ask your question and allow the answer to emerge whilst you rest. When using this approach, you have to be sure to let go of the question once it has been asked. Failure to do so can result in very disturbed sleep whilst the question buzzes around.

Expect Transformation

A couple of years into the new millennium, I was feeling uninspired at work. The projects we were attracting were tedious and price sensitive, and the clients seemed unappreciative and excessively demanding. I was beginning to wonder whether it was all worth it. I realise now I was in a place of acute desperation, and I believed that we had to take on every job that came our way.

I happened to come across a weekend workshop run by Nick Williams, author of several books, including *The Work You Were Born to Do.* The weekend was being held in the Lake District, a five-hour drive away, and it was winter. On one level, the thought of making such a journey did not appeal, but I intuitively wanted to go.

The workshop emphasised the importance of being inspired at work. We were asked searching questions around what had inspired us to start our businesses in the first place, what aspects of it we were thrilled by and wanted to do more of, and what facets we felt obliged to do but were bored by. During the course of the two days, I was shocked by what a rut I had got myself into. I resolved that I only wanted to take on projects I enjoyed, and to work with companies that were appreciative of what we did and were prepared to pay for it. I declared my commitment upon my return, and as an organisation we adopted it as a basic premise. We subcontracted the work that we did not want and took the companies off our database that we did not feel drawn to. Whenever I met prospective clients I did not feel good about, I made no effort to pursue them.

Getting clear on what you do not want and taking action is hugely empowering. You create the energy and time you need to focus on securing what you do really want. My enthusiasm returned, and within a few months I met two new clients who eventually became the cornerstones of our business. They were a quantum leap forward and provided rewarding, highly profitable work, and they were appreciative of our input.

When I say to others that we only work in areas in which we feel inspired, I often get the reaction that we must be in some sort of privileged position. They are convinced that they would not be able to apply such a strategy until they expand and are secure enough to be more discerning. This is not the case; focus and resolve come first. Only when you are clear and aligned with what you truly want can you start to attract it.

The Universe Always Assists

When we commit to nurturing and following our intuition and actively seek its guidance, our energy level and passion remain high, and we can expect real transformation in our lives. We still face problems, but overall we sense ourselves moving forward positively.

When we make mistakes, the universe does everything it can to turn our errors into learning experiences. Breaking my ankle was a painful lesson in the consequences of not heeding my intuition, but once I was severely hampered from going to work, I had lots of time to think. It was during this period that I had the inspiration to write this book, and a whole new life opened up as a result.

For Your Consideration

1. During what periods have you followed your intuition, and it has paid off?

_____

_____

_____

_____

_____

_____

_____

_____

_____

_____

_____

_____

_____

2. What are the best ways for you to develop your intuition (e.g. meditation, running), and how can you ensure you do these regularly?

_____

_____

_____

_____

_____

_____

_____

_____

_____

_____

_____

3. On what issue do you want intuitive guidance? Formulate your question, ask it as described above, and see where it takes you.

_____

_____

_____

_____

_____

_____

_____

_____

_____

_____

_____

_____

_____

_____

_____

CHAPTER 3

Vision Outperforms Planning

The Power of the Mind

Most of us go through the day taking little notice of our thought processes and how we manage them. Both positive and negative thoughts enter our heads all the time – they never stop. How we respond to them, and the degree to which we invest our energy in them, influence how we feel and the decisions we make.

In his book *Mind Power into the 21ˢᵗ Century*, John Kehoe explains.

> Everything in its purest and deepest essence is energy, and whatever you think, you are working with an immense amount of this energy in the quick, light, mobile form of thought. Thought is forever attempting to find form, is always looking for an outlet, is always trying to manifest itself. It is the nature of thought to try and materialise into its physical equivalent.

Most of us accept we are responsible for our lives, but we find it difficult to believe that we create our individual worlds at every level of existence. All our achievements and so-called failures are a result of our beliefs and predominant thought patterns. We even manifest into our lives the people we do and do not like, our successes and our financial struggles, and the good health or diseases we contract.

As each thought comes to us, we have the choice of pursuing it or not; this is free will. We all suffer negative thoughts, but if we are fully conscious, we simply witness them and let them go; they cannot take hold, and therefore they result in nothing. We are only trapped by negative thoughts when we identify with them and feed them.

Reflection on the past has obvious value, and it is hugely important to learn from our mistakes. When we face difficulties, it is useful to think of how we have solved previous similar challenges. On the other hand, excessive dwelling on the past provokes regret and ultimately depression. You sometimes hear people say, 'Well, in my day, we …' Then they go on to deliver a tedious monologue. Such comments are an indicator of being caught up in times long gone and disinterest in living in the present.

Robb, a loyal friend and one of the first to come forward and help me set up my restaurant, was somewhat prone to depression. One year, very tragically and within the short space of a couple of months, his mother, sister, and brother-in-law died. He returned to his mother's empty house and spent three months sorting out their affairs. He was very much alone at this time, and I imagine he went back in his thoughts to happier childhood days. Regret and remorse must have taken him over. According to his wife, he was never the same after he returned to their home in France. He went into profound depression, lost interest in his work, and took to alcohol. After a few years, he committed suicide by throwing himself into the River Seine. I suspect he was focussed entirely on negative thought. He must have convinced himself he was worthless and that his wife and two teenage daughters were better off without him. How else could he have justified the destruction of his own life and all the grief that ensued?

The ability to make a realistic assessment of the future is a great skill and some people are able to evaluate lots of conceivable outcomes from an impending decision relatively quickly. By contrast, too much concern about the future results in worry and anxiety, because we imagine all the different scenarios in which things can go wrong. The more we dwell on potential negative future outcomes, the more energy we put into creating exactly what we do not want. It's as though our thoughts, instead of being in free flow, get twisted and knotted and form a dysfunctional embryo. The more we continue to worry, the more we feed the embryo until it reaches a critical mass and becomes our reality. For those interested in understanding how thoughts create the chemical reactions that keep us addicted to patterns and feelings, including the ones that make us unhappy, it is worth reading Joe Dispenza's book *Evolve Your Brain: Breaking the Habit of Being Yourself.*

Our legal system is an area where worry about the future can be exploited by unscrupulous lawyers. Instead of helping two parties involved in a deal to see both sides of a situation in a realistic, balanced, and compassionate way, the system separates them out and obliges them to have individual solicitors. Both lawyers then ask all sorts of 'what if' questions that can unsettle their clients to the degree that doubt and suspicion creep in. Each individual 'what if' question is based on a fear of the other party failing to deliver on a commitment. Many of the 'what ifs' are extremely unlikely, even absurd, but when a whole stack of them get thrown at us, it becomes very difficult not to go into a state of disquiet and unease. The danger is that once such seeds are sown, not only can trust be seriously eroded, but we risk focussing so much on the possible disasters that we actually manifest them into our lives.

Spending too much time living in the past drains our energy and is distracting. We fail to see opportunities as they emerge and they pass by us. When we worry excessively about the future, it blocks the flow of life, insight, and vitality that is available to assist us in solving our next challenge. This is a lack of trust in life itself. Both extremes are destructive and cripple our effectiveness and creativity.

The Importance of Being Present

When we are in the present, we are alert and observant to what is happening not only externally but also internally – our feelings and any physical sensations we are experiencing. We are fully attentive, not absent in daydreams, and not distracted by fear, guilt, or regret.

The more we occupy the moment, the better able we are to hear and understand others, express ourselves, pick up on what is happening around us, and identify new options and opportunities. Our disappointments and anxieties effectively get squeezed out; there is no space for them. It is by being in the present that we reduce our levels of stress, massively improve our concentration, and enrich our lives.

The current upsurge in interest in mindfulness bears witness to our desire to live more in the moment. By paying attention to our breath, observing our thoughts and noticing how we respond to taste, colour, and different sounds, we become increasingly centred within our bodies. We flip less frequently into the past or the future and live in the present.

Recognising When We Are Not Present

Being able to identify when we are not in the present can be difficult; the busyness of life constantly nudges us out of it, and we do not even notice. How we feel is a key indicator. As a general barometer, we are not in the present when:

- we feel pressed for time and in a hurry

- thoughts buzz around our heads, and we fly from one thing to another
- other people irritate us unreasonably quickly and excessively
- our day does not flow: we call people and they are not there, our laptop freezes, or some other IT issue blocks us
- we forget things, lose time making good, and feel annoyed with ourselves
- we fully resolve nothing and feel frustration
- we go home feeling dissatisfied and exhausted

On the other hand, we know we are in the present when:

- we do not feel obsessed by schedules and are able to focus on whatever is in front of us
- difficult situations are resolved more easily than anticipated
- we are comfortable to take time out to talk to someone when it feels important
- we arrive late for an appointment and find whoever we are meeting has also been delayed
- we remember things just at the moment we need to
- we complete one task, enjoy a sense of completion, and move on to the next
- we feel trusting of others and able to deal with changing circumstances

Returning to the Present

Whenever you notice that you are not present, it is important to take a step back, give yourself a break, breathe deeply, slow down, and feel what is going on in your body. This in itself may prove sufficient to bring you back to the now. If it is not, observe your thoughts; see if there is something in particular that is upsetting you. Try to let go mentally of whatever it is, and resist pursuing and identifying with your thoughts. Put your attention on whatever is immediately in front of you and spend a moment appreciating what you do have. A degree of calm will return.

Next, select one simple thing that you are comfortable with and want to tackle; go to it and do it well. Focussing on one job to the exclusion of everything else will help significantly. When this is complete go to a second manageable task. You will know you are back in the present when you feel renewed confidence and are no longer preoccupied. Everything will again have a sense of flow about it.

My daily practice of meditation makes a significant difference to my ability to live in the now. It lessens the degree to which I get distracted by fear-based thoughts, and it roots me more solidly in my Higher Self. It is by being centred here that I build a bridge to Spirit and open up to what the universe has to offer. Eckhart Tolle summarises this place well in his book *Stillness Speaks*.

> In you, as in each human being, there is a dimension of consciousness far deeper than thought. It is the very essence of who you are. We may call it presence, awareness, the unconditioned consciousness. In the ancient teachings, it is the Christ within, or your Buddha nature. Finding that dimension frees you and the world from the suffering you inflict on yourself and others when the mind-made 'little me' is all you know and runs your life. Love, joy, creative expansion and lasting inner peace cannot come into your life except through that unconditioned dimension of consciousness.

Manifesting What You Want

Traditional thinking is that once you have a new business idea, you should write a detailed business plan and spell out what you intend to make happen over the next one to three years. I have produced and seen many such plans, and they are very necessary documents when looking for management buy-in or external funding. They are also useful in obliging you to think through the details of what you want to achieve and how you will get there.

On the other hand, some people get blocked and freeze internally when they start to dwell on all the potential hurdles they might have to face. This is a shame because they are focussing on the challenges in isolation. They project themselves forward to an imaginary time zone where they do not yet possess the resources and experience they will have, if and when such challenges emerge. Also, it is incredibly difficult to predict the future, especially beyond one year. Fast-evolving businesses move swiftly, new opportunities constantly unfold, and within weeks even the most thorough plans can be out of date.

Business plans will always have their place, but they will remain extrapolations of what we think the future might hold. As such, they are restricted by our experiences of life to date and the limitations of our logical minds. They can never incorporate those quantum leaps that come our way once we align with Spirit and allow the universe to assist us.

i) Clarifying the Vision

Assuming that we do create the world we experience, how do we go about creating what we truly want? The starting point is to get clear on the vision. When this is defined and passionately felt at a deep level, it inspires and lifts us beyond our current beliefs and perceived limitations; it acts like a powerful magnet that pulls to us what we desire. When we are totally aligned with our vision, and when what we want in our heads truly matches what we want in our hearts, the universe does everything it can to bring it to us.

If you want to open up a new market, launch a new product, or significantly expand your business, first define just what it is you want to manifest. Draw an image of your desired result and see it completed. Ensure your vision is exciting but not preposterous. It needs to move you in a powerful way and be ambitious, but you must feel that you have it within you to do it, even though it is a stretch.

Do not limit yourself by thinking you do not have the budget. Resist defining an exact time frame – it could come faster than you think – but do add the detail of who is involved and what it will look like. At this stage, you are not concerned with how it will come about.

This exercise is not a matter of producing a work of art. Whatever you come up with, it will be fully meaningful to you because you have created it. It has power because it comes from your very core, and you engage with that power by first making it manifest in the world in the form of an image. If you cannot draw, cut out appropriate pictures from magazines and make a collage. The important thing is to create a representation of your own dream in its entire splendour.

Next, make a habit of systematically revisiting the image. Position it somewhere so that you see it every day. Allow yourself to feel and enjoy the sense of excitement and satisfaction you would get from having accomplished your goal. It is by visualising and regularly connecting internally with the positive feelings of achievement that you programme yourself into a can-do attitude. It is by rooting the sense of success, by relishing the sheer unadulterated pleasure this gives you, that you build a confident attitude and override doubt. Many top sports personalities regularly use such an approach.

The universe wants to give us what we truly and genuinely desire, but if we insist on focusing on difficulties, lack of money, resources, or skills, then we end up amplifying those negatives instead. As Esther and Jerry Hicks explain in their book *Ask and It Is Given.*

> Whatever you are giving your attention to causes you to emit a vibration and the vibrations you offer act as your point of attraction. If there is something you desire, you put your attention on it and by the Law of Attraction it will come. However, if there is something you desire that you currently do not have, if you put your attention upon your current state of not having, then the Law of Attraction will continue to match that not having vibration.

By clarifying your dream in detail, making a habit of tuning into it, and feeling it successfully completed, you create a conduit through which things happen. You do not need to worry about how; the universe can bring things to pass much more elegantly and easily than you would ever imagine. What's more, it will often throw in a bonus, something extra that proves essential but was beyond your initial desires. Step by step, the way forward is revealed. You have to do your part, and it will be hard work on occasion, but revisiting the image regularly, helps sustain and re-inspire you through difficult periods.

When there were just two of us working full time in our market research business, my big goal was to make the transition from being an operation where everything depended on us, to a team of seven or eight. At such a size, I knew some of the larger clients we were targeting would feel more comfortable commissioning work from us. We had started to win regular contracts and had just purchased a first-floor office on a new business park, and we had space to accommodate more staff. I sketched seven to eight motivated people busy at work. They were enjoying themselves, and the office looked like a bright and cheerful place to be. I pinned the drawing up in the area where I got dressed in the mornings and made a point of looking at it and dwelling on it every day.

The evening news featured another impending recession, and other companies in our sector were struggling. Despite this, over the next three years we maintained growth rates in excess of 30 per cent per annum and expanded to a team of eight. I am not saying life was easy. There were plenty of challenges, but we dealt with issues as they came up, worked cohesively as a team, and enjoyed ourselves in the process.

During this period, the opportunity arose to buy the office below us. We took the plunge and purchased that too. The additional accommodation turned out to be the bonus. We could not have managed without it, because we needed space to hold meetings and receive guests. I had not envisaged this at the outset; I had thought one floor would have been plenty. The universe knew differently.

It would be too simplistic to accredit this success to an elementary sketch pinned on a bedroom wall. On the other hand, I am convinced that establishing a vision, externalising it, and revisiting it at the start of each day served as a constant reminder to my subconscious of what I wanted to achieve, and it helped keep me on track.

ii) Building the Day

I value meditation so much that I would not want life without it. It calms my mind; I get a sense of what is actually important and where my priorities lie, and I can let go of other issues that have been troubling me. Completely fresh ideas and new ways of seeing things emerge. Compared to starting the day by reading emails and allowing other people's requests and demands to become a priority, meditation puts me in charge. I am able to see where I need to focus, and I avoid getting involved in secondary issues that can be dealt with more effectively later in the day or by someone else. I start every day on my terms.

Towards the end of my meditation, I like to practise a few minutes of something I took from the Buddhist meditational practice of mettā. The goal of mettā is the cultivation of interpersonal harmony. It is the sending of love to ourselves, those close to us, friends, acquaintances, and finally those we find difficult. I bring to mind those people I have contact with during the day, especially the ones I am anxious about or in important negotiation with, and I visualise them surrounded in light. I find this appeases nervousness; my mind no longer actively feeds into worst-case scenarios, and I am less likely to manifest negative outcomes. As a result, the people I had apprehensions about show up surprisingly accepting and cooperative. Holding fellow team members in the same way also ensures I am joined with them even when I am not physically in the office.

iii) Being Congruent within Oneself

We are congruent within ourselves when our thoughts, feelings, words, and actions are fully aligned. This is a powerful state: our commitment and dedication inspire those around us, and we get things done. This is the place from where many successful entrepreneurs operate.

On the other hand, when we think we want something in our heads, but deep down we have unconscious conflicting feelings, we are incongruent. When this happens, we either attract something incomplete, nothing at all, or something detrimental. The unconscious is hidden to our daily thoughts, but it affects how we perceive things and the decisions we take. Independent of huge effort, our achievements remain lacklustre just as long as we remain incongruent and in conflict within ourselves.

Years ago, we decided we wanted to hire a sales manager. The idea was that I would focus my attention entirely on existing clients whilst he developed new ones – a strategy employed by many businesses. I started to put out the message that we were on the lookout, and someone I already knew came forward. He was an accomplished salesman who worked for one of our suppliers but was looking for a change. We went through the usual formalities of interviews and defining the role, and he accepted and came on board.

He spent the first few months understanding the business and then started to produce some positive results. He had a different style than me, and to my astonishment he would manage to set up sales meetings from very basic email invitations. By contrast, I had always spent hours on the phone introducing our services, sending tailored communications, and then offering a sales presentation. I was annoyed and envious of what he was achieving with so little effort. To me, he also seemed quite cavalier: he believed that once he had met people, if they wanted to do business with him, they would do so within six months – otherwise it would never happen. I took a more laboured view and had pursued some target clients for years.

After twelve months his performance dwindled to zero, and we were getting on each other's nerves. When I tried to raise the issue of underperformance, he retaliated that whatever he did, I would find fault, and it would never be good enough. I set very precise goals and objectives, but the problem failed to shift. I talked to other business owners and heard horror stories about how impossible it was to find decent staff. It was very depressing, and I was in a quandary as to what to do.

One day I said something that pushed him too far, and he stormed off. Two days later, we received a doctor's note saying he was ill and suffering from stress. After his entitlement to sick leave ran out, he resigned. It did emerge later that he had been agonising over various personal relationship problems, but I did not know the seriousness of his situation.

Some months later, I realised that winning new clients was actually my own passion. What I should have done was find someone to manage our existing clients and put myself in charge of winning new business. In my head, I wanted our new sales manager to succeed and prosper, but on an emotional level, I was resentful because I had given him the role I most enjoyed. Part of me was jealous and as such did not want him to succeed. I had created a situation that was bound to fail, and fail it did.

Incongruence can manifest in many forms. It will always be subtle, and sometimes it is never detected. If I had not realised how I was sabotaging myself, I could have gone on to hire another sales manager, and that person would have failed too.

iv) Being Congruent with Spirit

Congruence within ourselves is powerful and takes us a long way in business, but there are occasions when despite such focus things just do not work out. Whilst what we are seeking to manifest is what we want, it is not what we need and may even potentially be to our detriment. When this occurs, we can at first be extremely disappointed.

A year or two after we purchased and moved into our own offices, we won a couple of blue chip ongoing clients and grew quickly. I was feeling confident about future expansion – maybe even a little cocky. The purchase of our own premises had gone well, and we had plenty of space, but it was beginning to fill up. A further unit next door was put up for sale as a result of the previous owners going bankrupt. I thought we could buy it at a good price, knock through the intervening walls, and have more space available for when we needed it.

I went to my first auction at a slick hotel in Central London. My desired lot came up, and the auctioneer started the bidding at an unbelievably low price, just £1,000. Similar units had sold for £100,000 originally. The bids rose relatively quickly. At £20,000 there was only me and one other person at the back of the room involved. I really thought I was going to get it and expected the bidding to slow down, but it didn't. Immediately after I placed a bid, the other person made a higher offer.

Prior to the auction my fellow directors and I had decided that the maximum I would go to would be £30,000. In the excitement of the moment I went to £33,000 but then kept my hand down and dropped out. The lot went for £34,000 and the person at the back won the day. I went to see who it was, and to my amazement it was the original builder. He had bought back what had previously been his own property.

The story does not end here. Six months later, the unit was put back on the market because the builder had reneged on the deal. I interpreted this as a sign that the office really was meant for us and that we would get it at an exceptionally good price, less than £30,000.

At the next auction I saw no need to be personally present and opted to bid by telephone. Everything started the same, albeit there seemed to be more people in the bidding up £20,000. It then progressed surprisingly quickly up to £30,000 and there were still three active bidders. It reached £34,000, and I made a further bid, but the person relaying my offer over the phone either wasn't seen or didn't react in time. The auctioneer closed the bidding, and it had slipped through my fingers a second time!

At first I was perplexed and annoyed. It felt as though I was being conspired against. I was committed to the purchase, there was no problem raising the finance and everyone was behind the decision to buy.

Very much to my surprise and within just a week I had changed my mind. George, who later replaced me as CEO, looked more closely at how we were using our existing office and came up with a plan. He devised a new layout that not only improved our use of space but also provided plenty of accommodation for future staff. It turned out we had no need of the office next door. It would have been an unnecessary expenditure and potentially have made internal communications more difficult. This purchase was not meant to be. I had been congruent within myself but I did not get what I wanted. Instead, I received something we did need – a much improved use of existing space.

It is inspiring and energising to go for what we truly desire. Visualisation can help bring about the manifestation of our dream and being congruent within ourselves is essential. Nonetheless, there are occasions when we just do not know what is absolutely in our best interests. We have to let go of what we thought we wanted, and trust that whatever is appropriate, will emerge. Such moments can be distressing, but if we cling on to our old desires we become resentful and bitter and block positive movement. During such times it is our acceptance and faith that the universe holds something better that we **MUST** hang on to. In the case of the additional office it took a week for this to emerge. In more involved situations it may take longer. Such concepts require further explanation and the next chapters will elaborate.

For Your Consideration

1. During one half day, keep checking in with yourself to see whether your thoughts are fully in the present, or whether you are thinking of the past, worrying about the future, or daydreaming. If you notice you are not in the present, make a point of coming back to the moment. Pay attention to how this feels and whether it makes a difference. If it does, repeat it regularly.

_____

_____

_____

_____

_____

_____

_____

_____

_____
_____
_____
_____
_____
_____
_____

2. What is your big dream? Sketch it out or create a collage, and place it somewhere you will see it regularly. Explore how you feel with your goal successfully completed, and revisit your image daily.

_____
_____
_____
_____
_____
_____
_____
_____
_____
_____
_____
_____

3. In what aspects of your life do you feel fully congruent? Are there areas where you are not? Jot these down; you will receive insight as to why not, as you progress through the book.

_____
_____
_____
_____

_____
_____
_____
_____
_____
_____
_____
_____
_____
_____
_____
_____

CHAPTER 4

Transforming Self-Limiting Beliefs

Wealth Is Unlimited

A common misperception that underlies lots of people's thinking is that there is a finite amount of wealth in the world, and if one person enjoys abundance, it can only be at someone else's expense. If you compare the level of affluence in the world today to what it was just twenty years ago, you'll see how this is not the case. There are now over four hundred million middle-class citizens in China and India. This is more than the total population of the United States, and many of them are very wealthy indeed. This abundance was not stolen from the West – they created it. Quite simply, it was not there before. How can wealth be limited with this happening? We actually have the ability to extend wealth in spectacular ways.

A Benevolent Universe

I believe we live in a benevolent universe that seeks to give us so much more than we imagine. It wants us to fully achieve our potential, to overcome our challenges, and to blossom as individuals. When we do, we simultaneously become an expression of its goodness.

The life force that drives the universe has everyone's interests at heart. It knows the highest good of all, and in pursuit of it, we each have an important role to play. If we hold back and live only partial lives, we fail those around us. Abdication from life's challenges and the subsequent 'failures' we inevitably suffer feed negative belief and affirm fear. By acknowledging and appreciating the success of others, and by not dropping into jealousy and resentment, we open doors to our own success.

The life force never makes us do anything. We always have free will to do as we wish, but it does try to show us the way of our highest good. We are usually in alignment with it when we have a deep, ongoing passion to do something. You see this clearly in some children, who know that they want to become engineers, nurses, or actors. It's their sole aim and consumes them. Their drive can often be tracked back to an incident that triggered their imagination when they were young. Their attention is focussed, and they take in relevant information and naturally attract the opportunities they need in order to pursue their goals. Is it surprising when they excel in their chosen fields?

As a child, I did not experience such clarity of purpose, but I do remember a significant moment in the playground at school, when I was nine. Someone told me about a brass band that met above a local pub. I felt an urge to go and pestered my dad to take me. Fortunately he did, and the moment I entered the band room, I felt a sense of belonging, of being in the right place. The tutor, a coal miner and enthusiastic musician, produced an instrument for me and invited me to sit alongside the other kids in the junior band. I loved it, and within three years I was travelling and playing in concerts and competitions across the UK. I was mixing with adults who accepted and welcomed me. I developed a life outside of my parents' home, and I became independent much faster than I otherwise would. I remain thankful for that message from the playground. As children and adults, we are all given hints and directives as to what is in our true best interests. Sometimes we follow them, but many times we do not.

The Ego

Have you ever noticed that you are capable of resistance to your own success? It might start with an inkling you should do or say something, but then for whatever reason you block yourself. Later, you regret it. Alternatively, you agree to a course of action with which you are not totally comfortable, get side-tracked, and end up involved in something that is nothing like what you'd intended. Self-sabotage may seem absurd, but it frequently happens. We fail to follow our intuition, our personal programming and conditioning gets in the way, and we block opportunities from coming into our lives. In order to avoid falling prey to this, we need to better understand the workings of the unconscious mind and the ego in particular.

As small children, we are inherently enthusiastic about life. Everything is stimulating: food and sounds excite us, we want to touch and feel every little thing, and we are so eager for the next escapade that we run everywhere. Life is one big adventure as we seek to know where we belong and who we are in relation to those around us. The positive impressions and beliefs that we form during this time build our self-esteem and pride in ourselves. They become a central core, and as we grow, we draw from them the courage and strength to go out into the world and fulfil our dreams. This is the positive aspect of our ego.

The level of intensity with which we feel and learn as children not only encompasses the good times but extends to painful events too. During our early years, we are totally dependent on our parents; they are gods in our eyes, and we instinctively love them. We need their continued protection to feel safe, and if they are angry with us, it can be terrifying as we imagine they might abandon us. Our powers of cognitive understanding have yet to form, and we assume that whatever happened must have been our fault. The potential loss of their love and the safety they provide fills us with overwhelming fear.

We also attach enormous importance to the attitude of others. If a teacher or carer repeatedly insists we are stupid, we lose confidence and may decide we are incompetent. If a sibling seems to be always favoured, we feel inferior and may think we are unworthy and unloved. The continued repetition of these experiences at a susceptible age, and in particular the debilitating stories we invent around such events, build a detrimental and weak self-image. This is the other side of the coin, the negative aspect of the ego. It is made up of powerful and painful feelings, and we don't know how to express or deal with them. They terrify us so fundamentally that we push them deep down within ourselves, draw a veil over them, and pretend they are not there.

Our hidden fears and secrets sit there quietly until someone says or does something to reactivate them. It might be a completely neutral statement or act, but we take it personally, interpret it as attack, and respond inappropriately or clam up and fume. If we never seek the truth of what lies behind these moments and what we are making up around them, they have power over us. We react defensively and from a place of fear, and we make decisions we later regret.

As a small boy, I slept in a room next to my parents. The walls were thin, and the only way in and out was through my parents' bedroom. I could hear everything they said, and although I'm sure they believed I was asleep, I was introduced to sex before most of my contemporaries. The problem was I only partially understood what was happening. My parents were not at ease with their sexuality; I sensed their awkwardness and discord and resented being subjected to it. I felt betrayed but too frightened to object because that would have meant revealing I had heard what was going on. I fantasised about leaving home. Above all, I felt horribly trapped; I had no means of escape from the room and hated it.

For many years afterwards, whenever I sensed I was in any way restricted, my old, irrational emotions reactivated. That part of me that I had hidden and suppressed took over, and from a place of panic I would respond resentfully or angrily. Fear consumed me, I was possessed by my negative ego, my judgement was impaired, and I got myself into trouble. I never saw any of the positive solutions that were available.

We all suffer from negative egos, and we all experience circumstances that subconsciously remind us of memories that have caused us pain. We assume we are under attack, feel compelled to respond, and then later regret it. This is this negative ego; it holds us captive, creates disaster, and frequently results in self-sabotage and misery.

Our ego is a mix of positive and negative senses of identity. Our positive belief structures help us through life, and we access them with relative ease. The negative structures, on the other hand, are buried so deep they are hidden from our conscious minds. It is only after suffering the effects of them on many occasions that we eventually decide to look into them and face the cause of our distress.

The positive aspects of the ego have been acknowledged, and I propose to go no further into them. The negative aspects are hugely tricky, and we need to spend time examining their purpose and how to deal with them. Whenever I refer to the ego from now on, it will be the negative aspect.

Recognising the Ego

The ego is typically heard as a voice in the head. It brings with it a feeling of contraction, anxiety, and suspicion; it is never expansive, uplifting, or joyful. It is fear based, and so it craves safety and security. It never trusts, loathes risk, and seeks to compensate through control and manipulation. In the absence of self-worth, it seeks self-aggrandisement. It covets material things, lusting after money and more attention, but when these things are forthcoming, they are never enough and do not appease the underlying malaise.

The ego speaks from conditioning and misinterpretation of past experience. When triggered, it is very strong indeed. It judges and complains, thrives on separation, and enjoys misery because suffering justifies its negative belief structure. As the years go by, if never addressed the ego reinforces itself time and again. We become so entrenched that it completely envelops us. Would anyone consciously choose to arrive at this point?

In business the ego is very active around money, especially when it comes to what we are paid for our services. How much we make represents our value in the eyes of our ego, and if we feel underpaid, it resents it and makes a fuss. When pitching to new clients, this can be a minefield. There is no established trust, and if the prospective client is not willing or able to give an indication of their budget, it is easy to misjudge the price level at which to pitch the job. On the other hand, new clients are what we want, and provided we do not set too much of a price precedent, we are keen to give a competitive quote in order to win the business.

In the mid-1990s I pitched to be the principal speaker and organiser of an international conference in Scandinavia. This was the first time I had been asked to be involved at such a major event. I had to lead three key sessions during the day; Sue had to deliver a fourth, as well as brief and liaise with the supporting speakers. We viewed this as a golden opportunity to put us in front of two hundred potential new clients, and at the time we did not have many orders in the pipeline.

We put together a great presentation, but when it came to how much we should charge, my ego took control. I told myself I could not justify charging for preparation time; if I knew my subject, any preparation ought to be minimal. I also undervalued the time needed to brief and manage the other speakers, thinking it was just an administrative function.

Above all, I was desperate to win the contract because it was such a terrific opportunity.

I presented our proposals to the board of directors in charge of the Conference. Our suggestions were well received. I convinced them I knew what I was talking about and could engage their members' interest during what was to be the most important day of their year. Towards the end, they asked me how much I wanted to charge. I hesitated because I had no idea of their budget, and I announced one thousand pounds plus expenses. Much to my embarrassment they fell about with laughter; my quote was so hilarious they could not control themselves. They had expected to pay five times what I'd asked. They accused me of lowballing and I just wanted to disappear.

In this scenario I was dazzled by the glory of being a keynote speaker and the lure of potential business. I ignored the reality of what was involved and allowed my ego to undermine my worth. The net result was a gross under-pricing. Fortunately on this occasion, I got away with it. The directors did not assume I was totally desperate and probably incapable. They awarded us the job, and we were able to charge for some follow-up work. The event went well, but I regretted not making the money we deserved.

The Purpose of the Ego

The ego can never be annihilated. It is an integral part of us, and as such it needs to be accepted, acknowledged, and understood. Once we have the courage to face our fears, examine the false stories we have made up about ourselves, and let go of guilt, we no longer attract the situations that used to cause us so much grief. The people who used to provoke anger or irritation in us no longer do so because we see the Truth of who they are and no longer misinterpret their words or actions. We metamorphose the ego into a driving force, the dynamism we need to make things happen. Its negative energy is realigned in our favour, and we replace tendencies to self-sabotage with courage, confidence, and commitment.

A guy I once knew told me how, as a boy, he had been regularly and unfairly beaten by his father. The father would deliberately push him downstairs into the cellar and deliver crushing blows to his body and head on a regular basis. The boy was helpless; he didn't stand a chance in the face of such brutish behaviour. He instinctively made an incredibly courageous decision: he resolved that whatever happened, he would not cry. He was determined that his father would not have the satisfaction of seeing him break down. This in turn made the father even angrier, and more blows would ensue. I have no idea how murder was averted.

As the boy grew up, he had to deal with many feelings of being worthless, not respected, and unloved. In doing so, he found his purpose in life. He went into law and became a prominent defence lawyer. He simply could not stand to see injustice. He was so completely dedicated and driven that he took on many of society's unjustly accused and poorer citizens for no fee. He successfully transformed the pain of his childhood into the service of others.

The Integration of the Ego

We do not need to follow our ego voice. We can be our own masters, but not through suppression of the ego. It needs to be through its recognition, acceptance, and transformation into the service of our Higher Selves.

We all suffer egoic judgements every day, but there is nothing to be gained from feeling guilty about having such thoughts. They originate in fear, and we do not need to dwell on them. On many occasions it is possible to observe them and let them go. There are other occasions, however, when we experience strong negative emotions. We blame others for their inadequacies or feel angry about a situation we believe was not of our making. At times when our ego is triggered, our emotions take hold of us, and we are incapable of thinking straight and may even find it difficult to speak.

In such cases we need to resist the temptation to react in a knee-jerk way and play into the hands of the ego. We need to step back and ask in what way we are causing or contributing to the problem. What is the situation trying to bring to our attention, and what is it we need to learn?

In order to find the answers to such questions, we need help. Although there are many types of self-enquiry, the one I have found invaluable is the Clearing Process created by Sandy Levey-Lunden. When using this technique, usually with a partner who has been trained in the process, the dominant negative emotions are given full expression, no holds barred. The partner then uses a defined questioning technique to track back to the original source of the pain: what it was that gave the person such distress as a child. By working on an emotional level and using the prescribed formula of questions, the original source emerges remarkably quickly.

Once this source has been uncovered, it becomes possible to see the false stories we have made up about ourselves as a result of whatever happened in our past. Strengthened with such insight, the technique leads to genuine forgiveness of both others and ourselves. We understand the myths we made up around the original pain and how we have been recreating it ever since. After having worked through the process, we are able to let go of our self-limiting beliefs and see life positively and confidently once again. It was precisely this process which helped me understand my overreactions to sometimes feeling trapped, as well as why I felt so disempowered. By using the technique, I was able to uncover and unravel the source of the problem, forgive my parents, and see just how much I had been limiting myself.

Self-enquiry requires courage, honesty, and a willingness to go deep within. By committing and working it through, we transform the negativity of the ego into awareness, understanding, and personal breakthrough. Fresh ideas flood in, and we see options and solutions that were previously shielded from our awareness.

Self-limiting beliefs are certainly the biggest challenges in our business lives. There is no need to assess which are the most important, or indeed which ones to work on first; life will present us with exactly the right problem just as we need it. It will show up as a hot issue, and provided we address it first on an inner level, the breakthrough we need to deal with it on an outer level will emerge. As a result of such inner work, we create positive and lasting solutions, and our confidence grows. We understand that every problem comes for a reason, and there are no problems without solutions.

For Your Consideration

1. What were the passions you had as a child that you wish you had lived out?

_____

_____

_____

_____

_____

_____

_____

_____

_____

_____

_____

_____

_____

2. How could you now realise these dreams? What could you do that would give you equivalent joy?

_____

_____

_____

_____

_____

_____

_____

_____

_____

_____

_____

_____

_____

3. What issues, people, or situations wind you up to an excessive degree? Be honest, and make a note of these; you will gain insight into the causes as we progress.

_____

_____

_____

_____

_____

_____

_____

_____

_____

_____

_____

_____

_____

CHAPTER 5

Integrity and Trust Are Gold Standards

Dirty Business

The industrial revolution produced altruistic business owners who built homes, hospitals, and schools for their workers. In modern times, many entrepreneurs donate considerable sums to charity; they have a genuine desire to give something back. Such generosity is applauded, but there lurks an underlying belief that the very same benefactors could only have earned their money by riding roughshod over others at some stage. Such beliefs cast doubt over the integrity of all entrepreneurs.

Life in business is generally viewed as macho, cut-throat, and uncaring. It is not perceived as an environment that fosters trust, openness, and creativity. The behaviour of some bankers in recent years has further advanced the belief that business is purely about profit and greed. It would appear that there is little place for integrity and trust. Do we really want to continue in this vein?

The Value of Integrity

Integrity is an expression of wholeness in which people live out their values to their highest ideals. It is honesty and sincerity, and people with it show consistency between what they think, say, and do. They do not compromise themselves for easy material gain.

In business, integrity is a quality that shines through. Buyers feel safe around individuals of integrity and are secure in doing business with them; they know they will be respected. Many companies have mission statements stressing how important integrity is to them, but living it out under pressure requires real courage.

James was CEO of a design house. One of his key clients owed him a considerable amount of money and had recently placed a sizeable new contract. James had been pushing for payment, but it had yet to come through. The client had an arrogant attitude, and one day he arrived at the office and marched straight into the confidential area where James's staff were working on his project. He knew that this was off limits and that there was a distinct possibility he could have seen classified designs belonging to other companies. Worse still, he started giving direct instructions to the staff, going over the heads of their managers. James was informed of what was happening and decided that was enough. He had endured the client's pretentiousness for a long time, but this was too much. He confronted him, told him he had gone too far, and briskly escorted him off the premises.

Once the infringement had been dealt with, James wondered what the outcome would be. He had risked the loss of a key client. The current project could have been switched to another provider, and payment of the outstanding invoices could have been maliciously delayed. The client could have delivered a devastating blow that would have ruined the company.

To James's delight and relief, the outcome was the opposite. During ensuing visits, the client was respectful and honoured all boundaries. The project was completed successfully, and outstanding invoices were settled in a reasonable time frame. James demonstrated his absolute respect for his clients and his team. At a critical moment, he instinctively acted with integrity and enormous courage, and because he did so with total conviction, the outcome was successful. To this day the company is viewed as a quality supplier that can be trusted because it has such a high level of integrity.

CEOs with integrity always set the tone of their organisations. If the person at the top conducts their affairs with integrity, the rest of the team behaves similarly. People recognise it is the norm and live up to it. If, on the other hand, the CEO lacks integrity and deceives clients, fiddles expenses, or talks about others behind their backs, such behaviour is witnessed by staff, and they feel it is all right to behave likewise.

The lure of easy money is very seductive. When the situation arises, we are tempted to extend our boundaries of honesty, albeit just a little at first. The ego produces convincing arguments to justify our actions, but once we have stretched our integrity, it becomes easier to unroll it further.

We were commissioned to undertake a European research programme and had completed significant preparatory work. The first instalment had been paid, and we were waiting for our client to provide some necessary data. Despite requesting this several times, it never arrived, and the person who had commissioned the project changed roles and said nothing. This left me in a quandary: the money paid was significant, but I now doubted the work would ever get underway. What was I to do? My ego mind reasoned that because we had done so much at the outset, and because they seemed so disinterested, we were justified in keeping the cash.

Had this been a one-off, I would probably have left it there, but it wasn't. They were potentially an ongoing client, and whatever gain we had made was short term. This was brought to my attention quite suddenly at a trade exhibition, when I found myself in front of the company's stand. Exhibitions are excellent opportunities for making and reviving connections. My own contact was not present, but his replacement was. I was able to give my usual one-minute summary of our offering, but I lacked conviction. I felt awkward, something was blocking my energy, and I made no impact. I came away disappointed and perplexed.

On the flight home, I realised it was a sense of guilt that was thwarting me. I did not feel comfortable because I had not explained about the previous contract that his predecessor had commissioned and partly paid for. I had taken their money and delivered nothing. I knew I had compromised myself and was no longer coming from a place of integrity. Upon returning to the office, I emailed the new manager to explain what had slipped my mind, and we issued a credit note against their next project. I felt much better, and they were delighted. There was no longer any guilt blocking my energy, and the doors opened to discussions about future work.

The more we live with integrity, the more we attract clients with the same values. These are the ones we want. They are appreciative, pay their bills, do what they say they will do, and come back for more.

Honesty

To be honest is to speak the truth as we perceive it. We are all called to do this, but so often we shy away. We back off because we fear we might look foolish, offend others, or appear different. Successful businesses need leaders who speak their minds. Without honesty, fundamental issues are not questioned.

The ego also seeks to be liked, to be wanted, and to keep the peace, but our fear of offending others is frequently exaggerated. We imagine we might cause offence by challenging those with whom we disagree, but actually we help them clarify their own ideas and move forward in their thinking.

The ego never wants us to appear stupid or inadequate. It prefers that we remain silent rather than risk looking silly or inadequate. On many occasions, I have believed I was the only one not understanding something; then once I spoke out, I was amazed at how many others were in the same boat. Every time we ignore a query in our mind, a part of our brain closes down, and the more we allow unresolved questions to build up, the more we disengage and lose interest.

When presenting our own company, I find complete honesty around our skills and expertise is impactful. I explain what we do and why we are good at it, and then I go on to stress what we do not do and the reasons why. Clients are sometimes taken aback, but it helps them clarify precisely what our strengths are and in what situations they can use us.

Admitting Our Vulnerability

Being the boss is associated with being a strong individual, and although it is reassuring for others to be so, there are exceptions. We are all human beings; we make mistakes and get overwhelmed on occasion. Sometimes it is better to admit our vulnerability rather than put on a brave face, especially if this includes concealing significant truths. The ability to admit our vulnerabilities is a demonstration of our authenticity, and we gain respect for it when we do so. Those around us experience such sincerity as an expression of our trust in them. They feel drawn to us, and their loyalty is strengthened as a result. The ego, which always wants us to appear perfect, hates it.

When I realised it was time for me to move on from my restaurant, I was extremely anxious. I believed that if I made it known that I wanted to sell, my staff would become worried about their jobs, and motivation levels would drop. I might also have been perceived as betraying them.

Suddenly, everything came to a head. We were in a team meeting, and I could not contain myself. I became emotional, told them I wanted to sell the business, explained why, and said I felt I was letting everyone down. After a stunned silence, I was amazed: they completely understood and empathised. No one accused me of abandoning them. The sale became a joint endeavour, and there was no drop in energy or enthusiasm. All this stemmed from my being completely open and honest. By having the courage to allow myself to be vulnerable, I opened the door to others and allowed them to help me.

Trust In Ourselves

We demonstrate trust in ourselves when we do not feel we have to defend our identities. We do the best we can in a given situation and are comfortable in making ourselves vulnerable to potential disillusionment. Our interest is not in what happened so much as what happens now. If things do not work out, we pick up the pieces and move on.

We recognise that in business there are always situations and people that we need to take charge of, but we remain open to change and acknowledge when it is time to let others take over. We admit our fears but do not let them stop us from taking action. We allow our feelings to emerge rather than evading them, do the best we can to express them in the moment, and resist knee-jerk desires to criticise or belittle. After having stated our case clearly and without attack, we are able to take no for an answer.

As we develop trust in ourselves, we rely increasingly on our own inner wisdom and knowledge. We progress to a level of self-awareness where we are able to differentiate between 'in the moment' emotion, which calls for immediate positive response, and 'triggered' emotion, which is stirring something from our past. An example of this was James. He threw out the arrogant client who entered his company's confidential design area without permission. His anger at this infringement was entirely justified; he suffered no regret and a much improved situation ensued. Had he been responding from historical anger the outcome would have been very different; he would have suffered some form of negative outcome and remorse.

Trusting ourselves means opening ourselves up to resources beyond our restricted egoic view. Our self-esteem is bolstered, and our lives blossom as we learn to trust our own inner reference points and to live with uncertainty.

Trust in Others

We trust others when we can count on them to predictably and repeatedly deliver on their promises. We feel safe and secure in their presence, and we're confident with regard to the future. We believe we will not be damaged by them, at least not deliberately.

As David Richo explains in his book *Daring to Trust*, when we are young, our sense of trust is innocent, even naïve. Our expectations can be unrealistic, and if they are not met, we feel disappointed. Our egoic mind interprets this as betrayal and pushes us to take retaliatory actions. To a lesser or greater degree, we continue to operate from this level of trust throughout our lives.

Mature trust is when we maintain our faith in others even when things go wrong. We trust others to sort it out, and we have confidence that they will deliver the best possible solution. We resist judgement, condemnation, and attack, opting to maintain connection. We express our disappointment appropriately and proportionately, but then we let it go. From calmness we look at whether or not what was promised was actually in our best interests. Maybe what we have received is better. If we are fooled by someone, we learn from the experience, become more adept at setting boundaries, and move on. We grasp the futility of retaliation and choose forgiveness. When we come from a place of mature trust, people are comfortable with us; they are not burdened by unrealistic expectations.

Trust is a measure of our ability to live with uncertainty. It is faith that all will turn out for the best, even when we see no light at the end of the tunnel. By coming from scepticism and distrust, the ego nags us to cover our backs, fuss over detail, and pin down everything. It's naturally suspicious, and it persuades us to interfere with those to whom we have delegated responsibilities, making them nervous and undermining them. Their subsequent failure proves our ego's distrust, but ultimately we are the losers.

When we trust people, we reassure and inspire them, and they lift their game as a result. The more we are willing to embrace and trust, the greater the gift we give and the more we receive in return. We see practical evidence of this at Virgin, where the introduction of flexible working hours and holidays, and choice of work location have resulted in improved productivity and creativity. As Richard Branson says on his website.

> We at Virgin find a flexible working policy to be very effective. The guidelines, which we have introduced at almost all our companies over the past few years, effectively mean that as long as they do their work, our employees can work whenever they want, from wherever they want. It wasn't easy to put this system in place: Our team invested in research beforehand to make sure it was workable, and we had to encourage a change of culture across our offices. Yet that was a small price to pay, because it's what our employees wanted and we knew that demonstrating respect and trust in our employees, would boost their happiness levels, and in turn, their productivity and creativity.

Trust is always our best path, but sane discernment in how we place our trust is crucial too. When establishing business deals, we need sufficient checks and balances to define what will happen if things do not work out according to plan. Such controls need to be established from a place of openness, mutual understanding, and compassion. When conceived in fear and enforced by one party onto another, they are negatively loaded from the outset.

When clients buy from us, they put their trust in us; if we let them down, their own reputation is threatened. Trust has to be earned, and that takes time. At the beginning of a working relationship, people are not used to each other, and motives and actions can be misinterpreted. All the best clients I have worked with have initially presented us with challenges. It's as though there is a trust test that we must pass as a prerequisite to establishing a long-term relationship.

I attended an exploratory meeting with a German manufacturer of international standing. It became evident we were discussing an important project. A whole new product line had to be designed and developed, and the client needed to understand the target market in considerable detail.

The meeting went well. We submitted our proposal involving a series of focus groups with clinicians across Europe, and we won the job. The assignment did turn out to be a challenge. There were fewer clinicians fitting the exact profile of the type we needed, and it was difficult to find sufficient numbers to attend the groups. Also, the topic of discussion for the groups was complex, and we inadvertently recruited a number of inappropriate respondents. I apologised profusely, but I knew our patrons were beginning to question our abilities.

At such moments, one notices differences in national characteristics. When the English get upset, they rarely express it; they couch their words in diplomatic terms, and the gravity of the situation is not communicated. Germans, on the other hand, make it clear when they are not happy – they speak openly and explicitly. I feared if anything else went wrong, I would be on the receiving end of such Teutonic clarity.

The very next day, something else did go wrong. One of our normally much-appreciated interviewers floundered. She failed to moderate her groups skilfully. Maybe she was having a bad day, but this was the last straw for our client, and over dinner the issue came up. I listened to the complaints and acknowledged them; there was no point arguing. We were offered a deal. They would continue with us, but we would have to pay towards the next phase of the research from our own funds.

We could have agreed to take the hit and then cut corners to save on costs. Alternatively, we could have simply continued but been resentful during the remainder of the project. We did neither and remained totally committed. We used the insight we had gained to define realistic expectations during the next phase, and all went well.

The ego likes to take the easy way out, whereas integrity demands commitment. Our client saw how we handled the challenges. We did not seek to blame others, argue, or give up. Instead, we demonstrated a level of integrity that attracted them to us for the long term. We passed the trust test and went on to enjoy an extremely positive, ongoing relationship.

Trust can never be assumed. We all know how quickly it can be shattered. Even poorly worded emails can put valuable relationships in jeopardy. The reason for this fragility is that the ego is relentlessly suspicious, always lurking in the background and waiting to be activated. It is susceptible to misinterpreting situations in the face of incomplete information. It makes judgements and looks for justification to feel poorly done by or victimised. It is uncomfortable with connection with others and prefers separation. It is time and again at the root of loss of trust.

By contrast, people who have learned mature trust have stepped beyond their egos. It is a joyful experience and is always accompanied by creativity and high productivity.

For Your Consideration

1. In what situations has your integrity been tested? Assuming you exercised your integrity, what was your payback?

_____

_____

_____

_____

_____

_____

_____

_____

_____

_____

_____

_____

2. How honest are you with clients, staff, and suppliers? What are your fears around being more open with them?

_____

_____

_____

_____

_____

_____

_____

_____

_____

_____

3. Who do you trust most in your business life? Who do you trust least, and why? Note your responses and add any insights as you progress through the book.

_____

_____

_____

_____

_____

_____

_____

_____

_____

_____

_____

_____

_____

_____

_____

_____

CHAPTER 6

Forgiveness Leads to Freedom

Projection

'Projection' is the term used by psychologists to describe the process by which people hide aspects of themselves they do not want to acknowledge, instead attributing them to others. It is a remarkably subtle and involuntary ego defence mechanism. Its purpose is to avoid the fearful thoughts and feelings the conscious mind believes it cannot deal with. Rather than face what we perceive to be our negative traits, we blame them on others.

Projection demands effort. We expend energy in suppressing the aspects of ourselves we reject, but what we resist always persists. Just as excessive worry attracts the negative outcomes it dreads, projection draws to our attention people with the exact same characteristics we suppress. Debbie Ford explains in her book *Dark Side of the Light Chasers*.

> If we are uncomfortable with or deny anger
> we will attract angry people into our lives.
> We will suppress our own angry feelings and

judge people whom we see as angry. Since we
lie to ourselves about our own feelings, the
only way we can find them is to see them in
others. Other people mirror back our hidden
emotions and feelings, which allows us to
recognise and reclaim them.

When I meet new clients and find we get on, I'm
delighted. It's exciting to identify common interests. Should
they say something I do not agree with, I bear it in mind and
remain impartial. I even feel comfortable in joking about our
differences, and the relationship progresses unencumbered.

There are others I find problematic and even take an
aversion to. What they say annoys me; I experience difficulty
in expressing myself openly and end up putting on a show.
My negative reaction can be my intuition warning me not to
get involved. More frequently, I am projecting something of
myself onto them.

Projection is always accompanied by emotion, and the
bigger the projection, the stronger the emotion. We are invested
in our beliefs and want to be proved right. We take umbrage at
what was said or what we believe is implied by another, get into
an argument, and say things we later regret. Alternatively, we
hold back, say nothing, and come away feeling hurt, resentful,
and angry. In both cases, we lose objectivity, and our decision
making suffers.

Projection is inner denial and outer accusation. If I am
triggered and upset by someone I judge to be arrogant, what
is actually being brought to my attention is my discomfort
around my own arrogance. Maybe I had it drilled into me as
a child never to show such a trait, and I have viewed it as a sin
ever since, and have suppressed it. My denial might include
me presenting myself to the world as humble in an effort to
demonstrate I am not arrogant. Such pretence is futile, until I
face the arrogance in myself; the recognition of it in another
will continue to goad me.

In business, projection is frequently at the root of poor communication, and the higher up the management hierarchy it occurs, the more devastating the results. People avoid one another and fail to see each other's views. Misunderstandings and mistakes inevitably ensue, and people place blame on others. In extreme cases, projection appears as prejudice and bigotry, and that causes serious disharmony. When not dealt with, projection activates a sense of guilt and discomfort. We know deep down we are not being true to ourselves and are avoiding taking responsibility.

The good news is we are capable of sensing when we are projecting. We know that we do have a choice about whether or not to get sucked into the drama. The only people exempt from this are those who are so desensitised they are completely out of touch with their feelings.

At the moment the projection starts, when I am attentive, I notice that my mood suddenly changes. I become overly attached to my opinions, and I'm irritable and unreasonable compared to my normal self. If I voice my opinions to a third party, he or she does not share the extremity of my views. It is at this moment I need to pull back, go within, and ask myself what is at first a difficult question:

'What is this person reminding me of that is actually an aspect of *my own* personality that I do not like?'

A few months before we concluded our MBO, we decided to recruit a new sales and marketing director to replace me. We drew up a profile of our ideal candidate and began the interviewing process. I was able to draw from previous mistakes with the sales manager we had engaged about four years earlier, and we made sure we did not repeat them. Nevertheless, after seeing several applicants I started to wonder whether we would ever find someone suitable.

Finally Tyler arrived. He was keen, came across as very professional, asked searching questions, and had relevant experience. His marketing skills seemed strong, he had good ideas on how to take the business forward, and he presented himself well. His background was more pharmaceutical than medical devices, which concerned me a little. Pharmaceutical sales people can, in my opinion, be irritatingly slick. He had little direct working knowledge of market research, but over time we were all happy he would learn what he needed. On the whole, we were delighted we had found our man. We engaged him, and he started his induction period.

The plan was that Tyler and I would spend two to three months doing joint sales visits, and then I would step back and leave him to it. We did a couple of meetings together in the UK and then flew to Scandinavia to present our company to three key players in different cities. I had anticipated that by travelling together, eating together, and enjoying a drink after the working day, we would have time to get to know one another, and I looked forward to that.

Some people are very good at creating a positive first impression at interviews but turn out differently when appointed; you never really know what you are getting. Tyler was certainly affable, but I did not sense he ever relaxed, and I found it difficult to connect with him. Maybe as I was the outgoing CEO, he wanted to keep his distance from me.

I had asked him to organise the trip and book the hotels and transport, so when we landed in Copenhagen, he was more familiar with our itinerary than I was. He informed me that we were in a hotel in the city centre and should take a taxi. I knew the express train took only fifteen minutes from the airport, was much cheaper, and would be quicker. I pointed this out, and we took the train, but he appeared a little put out; maybe trains were not his style.

The next morning we set off to see the client. I led the presentation, and Tyler asked some good questions. He was extremely confident, albeit sometimes quite opinionated, and I noticed that his enquiries rarely led anywhere. He unsettled people but then left them hanging.

The client outlined the requirements, I suggested several ways forward, and we defined clear areas to follow up on. As we left their building, on our way back to the airport, I again suggested taking the train. Tyler got upset, stressed it was raining, and added that if walking to the station in his new thousand-pound suit damaged it, I would have to reimburse him. I pointed out it was only a slight drizzle, and he very reluctantly conceded, but I felt an unpleasant atmosphere developing between us.

I became increasingly angry with him as the day progressed. I began to see a prima donna with an arrogant attitude in everything he did. It was getting to me, and I knew I was in danger of overreacting. That evening I sat quietly and asked myself the question:

'What is Tyler reminding me of that is actually an aspect of *my own* personality that I do not like?'

I had to repeat the question several times. At first his diva attitude was nothing to do with me – it was all him! After a while, however, I began to realise that sometimes I have demonstrated similar characteristics. I was projecting on to him. If this had not been the case, I would have merely observed his manner, noted it, and not have been hooked into it. I asked where in my own life I was demonstrating the same traits, and a couple of incidents came to mind. I realised that when I had behaved arrogantly, it had been a cover-up; deep down I had been feeling inferior and inadequate. I felt humbled, and it dawned on me that Tyler was not the self-assured prima donna I'd judged him to be. He was hiding something from others and himself.

I was now calm and at ease, the emotional charge had gone, and I was able to observe him dispassionately. The insight I gained saved me from saying something I might have regretted. I stayed in charge rather than being taken over by an emotion that had me in its grip. In truth, we are all capable of being arrogant, and we have behaved so at some stage in our lives. When we fully acknowledge our potential to be so, we deal with it in others objectively. Ultimately, we are even thankful to whoever has appeared in our lives for bringing to our attention the very characteristic we needed to look at.

The benefit of owning and releasing our projections is that we unleash the energy previously bound up in holding our emotions in check. We feel empowered and free to express ourselves spontaneously. Misunderstandings and mistakes are avoided and those around us see our authenticity and want to engage with us. Is it surprising that new opportunities emerge?

Forgiveness

To forgive means to excuse or to pardon people for what they have done. It is to let go of resentment, anger, or hurt, wiping the slate clean. It is a compassionate act.

Unfortunately, it often comes in a temporary or conditional form. I 'forgive' someone, but in the back of my mind, I expect something in return and get upset if I do not receive it. Alternatively, I 'forgive', but as soon as the person upsets me again, I refer back to the original hurt. A further aberration of true forgiveness which is regularly practised but always camouflaged is one-upmanship. By being charitable and forgiving, I make myself out to be wonderfully magnanimous. An offender does me wrong, but I am big enough to forgive him. I get a sense of superiority from this, score points over him, and leave him feeling beholden to me. All such forms of forgiveness have little value, provoke resentment, and usually backfire.

True forgiveness can often be found through understanding. My sales manager prior to Tyler – the one who underperformed for six months – caused me no end of sleepless nights, but once I understood his situation, I was able to let go of my anger. His personal life was incredibly complicated, and had I been in his shoes, I would have been equally preoccupied. I still had to let him go because he wasn't doing his job, but understanding his circumstances made a huge difference. I knew why he had not been able to perform and was able to forgive him. There was no lingering resentment; we were able to work out a leaving package and move on.

I have heard it said that if we were to switch positions with people we judge, share their histories, and life experience, and endure their hurts, then we would behave in exactly the same way they do. I realise that this is a controversial statement. These days, when we hear about paedophile activity on the news, some amongst us are quick to condemn. Those who make such judgements are fortunate not to have experienced whatever it was that led those they condemn to their places of dysfunction.

It is by understanding the circumstances of a particular person's situation that we are able to separate the person from his actions. We do not condone what he has done. If he has committed a criminal offence, he has to pay the price, but through understanding the challenges of his life, we remember him as a human being. We gain a sense of compassion. The person has made poor decisions, and our acceptance that he has made mistakes, rather than committed evil, helps him deal with his own guilt. It gives the person the chance to take in what he needs to learn, and it inspires him to make good. This is real forgiveness, and it leads to true freedom for others and for ourselves.

Ten years ago, I came across and became a student of *A Course in Miracles*, a text channelled by Dr Helen Schucman between 1965–72. She was an associate professor of medical psychology at Columbia University and a highly respected figure. The Course's teachings echo the Buddhist belief that everything we see in our 'normal' world is an illusion, a kind of dream. We believe things happen *to* us and that others do things *to* us, but according to the Course, it is our subconscious attitudes and beliefs that draw to us situations and events in alignment with our thinking. What we believe is happening is not actually happening in Truth; it is a product of our subconscious. 'Reality' is to be found in that part of us that remains outside the illusion – our Higher Selves.

The idea that we are living out a dream is very challenging. Some of the experiences we attract in life are acutely painful, and to refer to them as illusions seems disrespectful, even insulting. I have certainly experienced challenging situations I believed were not of my own making, and I have felt misjudged and wrongfully accused. If I am completely honest, however – with the benefit of hindsight – I can see that inside me, there was some form of conflict, guilt, or projection going on. This was actually the source of my distress, and only by healing that could I let it go and find resolution.

The main theme of *A Course in Miracles* is forgiveness, and it includes a workbook with 365 lessons, one for each day of the year. As a student of the Course, I find that in awkward situations, provided I bring to mind the lesson, I begin to see situations differently and make better decisions as a result.

Forgiveness, as defined by the Course, includes the resolution and letting go of projection, and the acceptance that those who we believed were causing us pain are guiltless. They were just a part of our dream and came into our lives to help us learn something. In the words of Shakespeare, 'All the world's a stage, and all the men and women merely players.' Such people do us a great service. Can we really hold a grudge or be resentful of someone bearing such a precious gift?

The practice of the Course helps us understand that everything we experience is a lesson in forgiveness and that the best way we can help others is to see them as their Higher Selves. To see them as anything less means we buy into either their egoic thinking or our own.

At the airport in Copenhagen, while waiting for a return flight with Tyler, my ego took a serious bashing. I have always considered myself good at the consultative sale and accredit my success to good listening skills, an in-depth understanding of research, and many years of experience. I had anticipated that

Tyler would observe my particular style of presentation, take from it, and adapt it to fit his own personality.

I was in for a shock. Over coffee he abruptly announced he had learned all he needed from me and that he felt perfectly confident to take over with immediate effect! I went into shock. He had been on board for only a month. How could he be so impertinent? I had spent years getting to understand the business; I judged myself highly skilled and thought he could greatly benefit from my experience. Suddenly here I was, being told I was superficial to the requirements of the business I had created. I was outraged. Who did he think he was, making such a declaration?

A part of me wanted to fire him immediately, but I managed to bite my lip, made some excuse, and took a walk around the shops. I used a technique of forgiveness taught in the Course and said to myself many times over,

'Spirit is the love in which I forgive Tyler. I release my
negative thoughts about him into the hands of the
greater good and ask to see the situation differently.'

I made sure I stayed with the emotion of what was going on inside me. I breathed deeply, and kept repeating the declaration, and did my best not to feed the fury that was going on in my head. After some time, a degree of calmness came; my anger started to reduce and no longer totally possessed me. Then, after even more repetition, a new way of seeing the situation started to emerge. For the first time ever, I realised that although work had been a crucial part of my existence, it was not the totality of who I am. I knew I wanted to complete the MBO and leave the business, but I had not considered my life thereafter. I began to grasp that although I was coming to the end of this phase, something quite liberating might be around the corner, if I could embrace it. I even began to see the funny side of Tyler's statement and how I had reacted. I laughed out loud and returned in an entirely different frame of mind.

Thanks to Tyler, I was able to start disengaging emotionally and physically from the business sooner than I had anticipated. Deep within I knew it was time to move on, but in my egoic mind I was loathe to leave, and I suspect I would have invented all sorts of reasons to linger. I needed this incident to crowbar me out and free me up to move in a new direction. I felt genuine excitement at the thought of opening up to something new, and I realised I had attracted Tyler into my life to help me grasp this. He had played his part well, and I am grateful he did.

A few months later, after I had left the business, Tyler was in fact fired. He proved not to share the values of the rest of the team, shut himself off, couldn't work with George (the new CEO), and failed to deliver on his promises. In his first days he seemed to everyone to show clarity, focus, and glamour, but he revealed himself to be loud, confident, and wrong. It was actually a huge relief to everyone when he left, and once the energy in the office settled, orders flowed in again positively.

Self-Forgiveness

When someone apologises sincerely to us, we are keen to forgive and forget. So much hurt can be appeased by just a few honest and heartfelt words. Forgiving ourselves, on the other hand, is more of a challenge. We judge ourselves very critically, and despite being told by others we are not to blame, we continue to hold ourselves responsible and beat ourselves up.

Forgiving others is based on the realisation that they are fundamentally innocent and have come into our lives to show us something, and self-forgiveness is the same. Whatever we have done that we feel guilty about, it was just a mistake. It was not something evil for which we must be forever condemned. If we have committed a criminal offence, we need to pay the price, but within our Higher Selves we remain pure and guiltless. The realisation of this sets us free to make amends where it is appropriate and to go forward with wisdom and compassion.

Habit and fear are the biggest barriers to self-forgiveness. In a perverse way and at a subconscious level, we become so accustomed to guilt and living in fear that the thought of moving out of our personal hell terrifies us. We become the sad prisoner who has been incarcerated for so long he can no longer think for himself or take any responsibility, and he prefers instead to stay locked up.

It is essential to understand why we make the mistakes we do because this helps us avoid repeating them and assists us to grow in our acceptance and understanding of ourselves. Once we have mastered whatever the lesson is, the universe wants for nothing else but to give us a second chance. Our Higher Selves know we are innocent, and the relinquishment of guilt takes us back into alignment. By comparison, holding on to guilt serves only our ego – it is actually a debilitating and selfish act. It keeps us locked into feelings of being unworthy.

Forgiveness of oneself ultimately depends on a personal decision to change. The ego can always find reasons to hold back and remain in guilt, regret, or feelings of unworthiness. I have known people who have been through years of therapy and still remain stuck. We all have free will and can remain locked up in our personal hell all our lives, if we so choose. For those suffering severe depression or mental illness, it may not be possible to make the change, but most of us can. However, we must be prepared to leave what we have grown accustomed to, and rather than remaining victims, take the risk and reveal our true identities.

The unforgiving mind always remains in despair. It is convinced it is right and rarely opens up to suggestion. It attaches mistakes to people, makes them wrong, and judges and pronounces them guilty. By contrast, true forgiveness restores peace and allows abundance to flow. Every time we choose to work on ourselves instead of projecting blame, we arrive at forgiveness and experience freedom.

For Your Consideration

1. Be observant with yourself over the next few days. See whether you get unduly upset by the comments, actions, or the perceived manner of another.

_____

_____

_____

_____

_____

_____

_____

_____

_____

_____

_____

_____

_____

2. Consider 'What is this person reminding me of that is actually an aspect of my own personality I do not like?' As your answers surface ask where in your own life you are demonstrating the same trait.

_____

_____

_____

_____

_____

_____

_____

_____

_____

_____

_____

_____

_____

_____

_____

3. Say to yourself, 'Spirit is the love in which I forgive. I release my negative thoughts about …(the other) to the greater good and ask to see the situation differently.' Note any new ways of seeing the person and the situation.

_____

_____

_____

_____

_____

_____

_____

_____

_____

_____

_____

_____

CHAPTER 7

Self-Empowerment

We are empowered when we live physically, mentally, and emotionally in alignment with the Truth of who we really are. We recognise we are empowered when we feel comfortable standing by our opinions and speaking authentically, but we have no compulsion to be dictatorial. We do not tread around others as if on eggshells, and when we disagree with someone, we speak our minds without aggression or resentment. We enjoy a sense of being connected to those around us, see beyond their limitations, acknowledge we do not know it all, and appreciate feedback. In particular, we do not take ourselves too seriously and are comfortable in play. We respond to the moment and observe that those around us take notice and want to engage with us. We live out our destinies and inspire others to do likewise.

We are disempowered when we allow self-criticism, self-chatter, and victim thinking to dominate our thoughts; as a result, we hold back, feel suppressed, and are afraid to engage. Our egos never have our happiness at heart and struggle relentlessly to keep us in a vice-like grip, too frightened to venture out beyond our comfort zones. Every time something is said that could be misinterpreted, our egos do so and use it to affirm that we are unworthy, guilty, or inadequate. Our egos constantly keep us thinking in a way that is opposed to our real selves.

We start life carefree, trusting, and innocent, but as the years go by, if our egos have their way, we become critical, complaining, disinterested, and miserable. Unresolved feelings of guilt draw us to depression, we hide from contact with former friends, and we fail to recognise the kindness of others. Such is the goal of the ego. It has its way with all of us some of the time, and far too many of us most of the time.

We further disempower ourselves when we are judgemental, fail to express our real selves, and dwell too long on dramas and situations we cannot influence. Every time something happens to trigger us, and every time we suffer an experience we fail to deal with satisfactorily, we experience disempowerment.

In order to express ourselves without fear, to thrive, and to live in an empowered way, we need to establish patterns of living that reinforce our positive state.

Challenge the Workaholic Within

There is plenty of evidence these days to show the personal costs of being a workaholic. Air travel, switching time zones, disturbed sleep, stress, lack of exercise, and irregular meals deplete our strength and contribute to the chances of suffering illness and disease. The cost to our personal relationships – not spending quality time with our partners, or not being around for our kids – takes us closer to estrangement and isolation.

Entrepreneurs do need to put huge dedication and hours into their business, and working nine to five Monday to Friday is not a practical option. In order to keep our enthusiasm fresh over the years, it is essential to resist thinking that we have no time for ourselves. We must define what it is that replenishes our Spirit, as well as our physical and emotional beings. We need to challenge where we are putting our focus and make our own well-being a top priority.

Nurture the Physical Body

We are so much more than our physical bodies, but they are the means by which we communicate and function in this world. We should never be obsessive about our own body, but it does need to be respected. When we nourish and care for it, we do not engender unnecessary illness and pain, and it serves us for many years as a result.

A good diet is important. Personally, I much prefer organic, fresh, and (where possible) locally grown foods. I am not vegetarian or vegan, but I rarely eat red meat; I simply do not feel drawn to it. Green vegetables are excellent as long as they are not overcooked, and wherever possible I avoid processed foods. I find travelling, especially air travel, quite challenging. The food you find in some airports, planes, and hotels can be far from wholesome, and after a week of it I can feel myself becoming stodgy, even lethargic. Whenever I can, I actively seek out nutritious food in restaurants where the meals are freshly cooked, not microwaved. Failing that, I head for the nearest Italian restaurant.

I do now drink lots of water. I used to be very prone to falling asleep around 4.00–5.00 p.m. Such an inclination to nod off can be dangerous, especially if driving. By contrast, provided I do drink enough water (up to two litres per day), I feel much less sleepy in the late afternoon.

When something absolutely essential comes up, and I am fatigued late in the evening, I do my best to solve the issue wholeheartedly, and as a result it normally comes to a successful conclusion. I can then put it to one side, go to bed, and sleep peacefully. However, I have to be careful to check that I am in the right frame of mind. If I begrudge getting involved, the situation deteriorates, and I tend to make matters worse.

As an entrepreneur, holidays can prove difficult to schedule, and when you finally get there, it takes a couple of days to unwind. My parents ran their own grocery business. They opened five and a half days per week, and when the shop was closed, people came to the back door. They believed one of them needed to be present at all times and never went on holiday together. This was a great shame because it did nothing for their relationship. I am convinced it contributed to my father going to an early grave at the age of forty-eight. He achieved his ambition of running his own business, but he spent his life being a servant to it. He epitomised the entrepreneur who found the work he loved but failed to get his work-life balance right, and he suffered the consequences.

These days, because everything moves so quickly and communication can be instant, many entrepreneurs resist going on holiday because they dread the mountain of emails they face on their return. This is a real challenge. For myself, I know that if I spend time looking at emails whilst supposedly on holiday, and I try to respond only to those I believe important, I inevitably get drawn into more than I intended. I risk interfering with what others are doing and either make or precipitate poor decisions based on partial information. This is frustrating for all, and I get to the end of the holiday feeling resentful that I have not had a proper break.

The best way to ensure we get the break we deserve is to:

- Leave clear instructions in an automated email response to specify who to contact whilst we are away, including name, telephone number, and email address. The reply needs to explain that we are on holiday and say on what date we will return. When clients or suppliers know we are on vacation, they prefer not to disturb us, but they do need an informed contact to talk to.
- Whoever we name needs to be as fully briefed as possible and encouraged to make decisions and not

postpone them. Where essential, if they really have an issue they are uncomfortable with, they should be able to let us know and ask for help. This request for communication is best initiated by SMS or a phone call, not email. The contact must come from the person we left in charge, not from us calling in or emailing to check how things are going. This is a great exercise in trust because we have to be careful not to take over the situation. Personally, I have always been amazed at how well people rise to the responsibility of being in charge. Their confidence grows, and they provide real proof that we can take time for ourselves.

- Upon our return from holiday, we must set our expectations at a reasonable level and allow at least the first day to be debriefed on what has happened and to read and prioritise emails. It's best to avoid getting involved too quickly in order to give ourselves time to get a balanced picture before we start making proactive decisions.

There is no point in becoming a slave to the businesses we create. Balance is critical. Yes, there are times when it is necessary to work long hours. Yes, we will work weekends more often than we would like. But we must never get stuck in thinking that we have no choice. Creating proper time for ourselves starts with a conscious decision and the resolve to make it happen. Even when working long hours, it is possible to maintain a degree of equilibrium, but we do have to want to achieve it.

A good balance for me includes:

- Not looking at a computer screen after 9.00 p.m.
- Only watching TV programmes that genuinely interest me
- Reading something uplifting for ten minutes before sleep

- Nutritious food and up to two litres of water per day
- Thirty minutes of exercise three times per week
- A minimum of two weeks holiday plus three to four long weekends every year

Practise Meditation

Our biggest barrier to success in life is the continuous negative chatter that goes on in our heads. Our inner critics are our worst enemies. We tell ourselves stories about not being good enough, being undeserving, or being limited all the time. Such destructive thinking is relentless.

The beauty of meditation is that it releases the grip of negative thought and self-criticism. We regain the power of living in the present and reverse the effects of stress. We reconnect with our Higher Selves and begin to see positive alternatives that we could not have previously contemplated.

The regular practice of meditation also has compelling health benefits: it has been proven to reduce stress and blood pressure, and increase concentration. The trouble with modern medicine is that it takes the responsibility for our health out of our hands. Many doctors prescribe beta blockers or equivalent medications to slow down the heart rate. Meditation achieves the same result quite naturally – and without the side effects. Meditation also significantly strengthens the immune system. I rarely get a cold, and when I suffer anxiety and sleeplessness during the night, I turn to meditation to calm my thoughts, let go of the anxiety, and fall into a relaxed sleep.

There are many forms of meditation, and so if one form does not suit, another will. A beginner might think it is complicated and may postpone getting involved, but this is the ego getting in the way. Meditation seriously unseats the ego, which will always do everything it can to resist.

My own preference is to sit quietly for twenty minutes as soon as I am out of bed and dressed. I like to read something uplifting to start the day, and so I begin with the Course lesson for that day. I then sit quietly, observe my breathing, and let my thoughts go. Letting go is not easy, but with practice it becomes more natural. As I quiet my thinking, I sense relief and observe myself becoming calmer and more present. My breathing imperceptibly slows down, and I experience a sense of peace. The thoughts do not stop altogether, but they become less frequent.

It is in this place of emptiness, of "egolessness", that I become aware of my Higher Self. It is from this place that new understanding and ideas come to me. When such insight is revelatory, the temptation is to pull out of the meditation and make a note, to avoid it being forgotten, but it's best to resist this and continue. The gems will still be there at the end.

Some entrepreneurs argue that taking time out for meditation is well and good, but they simply do not have the time. That statement could not be further from the truth. Meditation is actually time saving: it enables us to see what is really important and what is not. It is definitely a challenge to include meditation in your routine. If you have to get up at 4.00 a.m. to get to the airport, or if you have young children who are awake at dawn demanding attention, then finding time to meditate is a challenge. It is essential to find the time when you can. Unbeknownst to anyone, I have spent many hours meditating in airport lounges, on airplanes, and on trains. People assume I am asleep and leave me to it. It is very easy to make excuses as to why meditation is impractical. Recognise the resistance and do it anyway.

Do What Inspires You

For some entrepreneurs, the generation of money is the entire focus of what inspires them. They can have several fingers in different pies, and as long as each of the businesses with which they are involved is making a good return, everything is fine. Such entrepreneurs have an ability to see the big issues in a business, and they can pinpoint what needs changing to improve productivity, rationalise supply, or leverage marketing. Provided they focus on sectors they feel comfortable in, they can get involved quickly, make their contribution, move on once the job is done, and take their just reward.

For others, their businesses are centred on a particular passion, something they especially enjoy. This might be tourism, fashion, or fishing. What is important is that wherever the passion lies, the business is built around it. For myself, I have always been interested in enquiry and understanding why people behave the way they do. Market research lends itself perfectly to this.

Whatever type of entrepreneur you are, the achievement of abundance can only be realised if you are doing what inspires you. To live in abundance means to be entirely happy. If you are not following your dream, happiness will elude you.

If I'm not working with inspiration, I get tired and frustrated, and everything becomes an effort. When I work with inspiration, I am able to sustain long periods of exertion, view problems as challenges to be overcome, and take pleasure in finding solutions. When I follow my inspiration, I notice that I draw in others who share my enthusiasm and enjoy being alongside me.

During the early 1990s, we were mainly involved in marketing consultancy. We assisted firms of accountants with an interest in the medical sector. GP practices were growing rapidly, building custom designed premises, incorporating pharmacies, and offering complementary services. They were becoming significant businesses in their own right. It was a truly dynamic time, but the majority of doctors had no idea how to manage the transition. There was huge potential for those accountants with relevant expertise to offer proactive advice.

However, the accountants suffered a major weakness: they had no idea about marketing. Even the basic concept of building a database was alien to them. We pitched and won a job to put together a marketing plan for a small accountancy practice, and then we helped them package up and market their specialist offering. They became surprisingly successful at winning new business and were obviously delighted. This in turn gave us huge satisfaction and an excellent financial return.

After having been through the process for one firm, it was comparatively straightforward to roll it out to others. We offered our services on an exclusive basis, only working for one firm per geographic area. We won clients nationwide and became the go-to marketing agency for a newly created network of specialist medical accountants across the UK.

One major limitation emerged. Once we had worked with a given accountancy practice for two to three years, they achieved a position of dominance in their region, and we had worked ourselves out of a job. We became redundant.

We made a logical extrapolation. We assumed that because we knew all these firms of accountants, and because they also needed help marketing themselves to small and medium-sized businesses (SMEs), we could be of assistance on that front too. In theory this made sense; we had the contacts and the credibility, and it was simply a matter of introducing our services to other departments within the firms we already knew.

The reality proved remarkably different. SMEs are wide ranging by business type, and there was no common denominator of change underway to which the accountants could add value and differentiate themselves. We had some success, but we made poor progress. Our focus had changed from an exciting sector where we made a major contribution to one where everything became a struggle. Our lives transitioned from being inspiration based to drudgery dominated, and it happened in a relatively short space of time.

It was during this period that Sue took a step back and asked herself what we needed to learn from the situation – what it was we needed to do differently. I am delighted she did, because I was too engrossed in survival and paying the bills. She suggested we drop the whole accountancy sector and look elsewhere. The thought terrified me, and my ego felt hugely threatened. She also pointed out that on the market research side of the business, which still existed (albeit in a minor way), we had just completed an interesting project in medical devices. She suggested we pursue that.

I saw the value of what she was saying. We let go of our work with accountants over the next few months and immersed ourselves in the medical device field. This was a bold step, but it rapidly proved to be an immensely positive decision. We both felt an affinity for the products, we liked the people, and the market was international and enjoying long-term growth. We returned to inspiration, and our work once again had real purpose. I travelled regularly across Europe and the United States, as well as South America, Africa, China, and India. We never suffered a bad debt, and we enjoyed growing the business over a fourteen-year period before we eventually moved on. All this could only have happened because we followed what inspired us.

Work with Clients You Like

Abundance comes to those who excel, and you can only excel if you enjoy working with your clients. If you do not genuinely like them, your disinterest will eventually show up, and you will be at risk of them finding someone who does.

There is much talk in traditional business textbooks about the importance of adding value in order to differentiate one's product or service and to build brand loyalty. This principle is certainly crucial, but it lacks an important note of caution. Adding value requires willingness to go the extra mile, and it is difficult to do that in a sustained way with people or organisations for whom we do not have genuine affection. If we are not aligned with someone, our negativity, however subtle, blocks the creativity and energy we need in order to consistently add value. On the other hand, when we genuinely like someone, we find ourselves quite naturally wanting to help them, and our creative energies flow. I make it a rule to work only with people with whom I genuinely want to work, and I have done so since before we had a regular ongoing client base.

I first met Julian when his company and ours were working on a joint project; he has a leading role in a product development company. I enjoy his enthusiasm, his openness, and his ability to think outside the box. He had an ongoing requirement to test prototypes, and he did this by travelling around, demonstrating the prototypes to family and friends and asking their opinions. He was quite happy with the results he achieved, but we suggested it would save him time if we could organise the recruitment of people off the street and present them to him at thirty-minute intervals in a nearby, convenient location. Such a task is quite straightforward if you have the resources, but Julian did not – and furthermore, he did not want to get involved in such a process. He quite rightly wanted to concentrate on what he did best, the testing and development of concepts, and I happily organised this recruitment for him. It was a good deal for everyone, and we repeated the exercise several times.

Later on, we were asked to recruit specialist nurses and patients with particular diseases such as Parkinson's and rheumatoid arthritis. Normally I would not involve myself in this; such recruitment is project management driven and requires a detailed eye, which is not one of my fortes. Also, when it goes wrong, it can be an all-consuming nightmare, and one has to drop everything to sort it out. However, because it was Julian, I did get involved. I forced myself to pay attention to the detail and was happy to do so because I genuinely wanted to help him. Also, due to my specialist knowledge of the sector, I was able to add value to the thinking behind the projects.

After a year or two, the geographic requirement expanded. We were asked to do similar recruitment in France, Germany, the United States, and even Australia. Fortunately, we already had a network of people to do this type of work for our own purposes, and so we were able to make use of them. At all stages, whilst Julian was directly involved, I remained on the case. The demand for his service grew massively. He took on a team of people to keep up and his company is now a leading player in the field. I like to think that we made a contribution to his success. The company's involvement with us grew from several thousand pounds to several hundreds of thousands a year.

This highly profitable result was born out of the positive relationship between Julian and me. There were many challenging moments en route, but because of the strength of the relationship, we always knew we could resolve anything that came up.

Empower Your Initial Bid

Established clients understand the value we add, and assuming the relationship is based on trust, it is relatively easy to discuss and negotiate on price. If we lose on one project to accommodate our client, we know we will gain on another.

The situation is different with new clients. Trust has yet to be established, the ego is hyperactive, and there can be lots of opportunities for misunderstanding. I have attended many initial meetings, thought I had understood the requirement, eagerly submitted a written proposal, and suffered rejection. In these situations, I have either over or underestimated the importance or complexity of the project, and I incorrectly pitched the price. This is not an unusual mistake, and it is not due to clients consciously holding back information. It is because certain issues have yet to emerge in the client's consciousness, and budgets have yet to be properly thought through. Full communication and understanding rarely coincide at a first meeting.

When I submit a significant proposal, I do the best I can to build in a face-to-face meeting to present my bid. This applies even if it means taking a flight and spending a day travelling.

This second meeting provides me with the opportunity to explain our logic and allay any misunderstandings. I can delve deeper into the client's real needs, adapt our approach to match the fuller picture, and set expectations at the right level. It also provides the opportunity to create meaningful bonds and test budgets.

Respect Your Own Value

There is often a tension with new clients between winning the work and going in too cheaply. By cutting our prices, we believe we stand more chance of winning the work, but the risk is we set a precedent and never make the return we deserve.

We once pitched for a project to host an international focus group in South Africa with specialist clinicians from around the globe. We won the job, but only after dropping our price significantly. It was made clear that if we wanted the work, we had to do it on their terms. I felt uncomfortable with this but reminded myself that this was a client we had wanted to win for a couple of years, and the discount was worth it to get them on board. I flew to Cape Town and did the job myself. It went well, and I felt we had made a positive impression.

A couple of months later, we were asked by another department within the same company to do a similar project in France. We submitted our proposal, and it was accepted – but only on the condition we included some rather demanding extras. Changes in specification usually merit a price increase, but once again they refused to accommodate. In addition, we were asked to invite as many of the delegates as possible to stay on after the focus group and join our client for a dinner in the evening. This was an unusual request. During the process of research, clients normally prefer to remain anonymous. My intuition was ringing alarm bells, and the situation kept deteriorating.

The day of the event arrived. We experienced some technical hitches with sound transmission, but we sorted them and were ready to go. Unfortunately, two of the eight clinicians suffered delays and arrived late, but we did accomplish everything we had promised. To my mind, the late arrival of the two participants made no difference to the quality of the work done.

Our client took a different view. In order to compensate for the late arrivals, they requested that we pay for the dinner. It was made clear that if we did not, we would never work with them again. It was not a huge amount of money, approximately two thousand Euros, but I was furious. I dug my heels in and refused.

In the days that followed, I questioned myself many times as to whether or not I had done the right thing. One should never close the door on a business relationship, and I had slammed this one shut. My intuition told me I had done the right thing, but my head cursed me for losing a client for the sake of two thousand Euros.

Should I have done things differently? I doubt it. This was a client that was unlikely to ever value our services. Had we caved in and paid for the dinner, the pain would have repeated itself in some other shape or form. We must respect our own value. If we do not honour ourselves, others never will either.

The previous example is an extreme case. I have had many other experiences where we have given a discount initially and then later were able to justify charging our usual rates. It is always a matter of convincing the client of the value we add. Sometimes this can be done upfront, before any projects are commissioned; sometimes we have to demonstrate it as we go. The key is to respect our own value and have confidence in our own worth.

Delegate or Let Go

The quality of the relationship is critical to business success, and when bad feeling starts to arise, it is essential to first look inwardly at whatever projections we might be making. That said, there will always be some individuals with whom we never click. In these cases, it is far better to recognise the barrier and hand them over positively to someone else. This is not a sign of weakness; it's being practical. The worst scenario is to do nothing.

Steve was the European marketing director of a diagnostics company, and I had enjoyed an excellent relationship with him for about four years. On his instigation, we had developed a bespoke research programme from which his team had gained huge benefits. Such was the level of trust he had in us that he rarely asked for competitive quotes, and only when formally obliged to do so. The time came, however, when he had to move on and delegate responsibility for research to someone else.

He appointed Maureen, an extremely competent young lady, and I went to meet her. To be perfectly honest, deep down I resented her arrival. I viewed the programme as 'ours', and when she announced she wanted to update it and make all sorts of changes, I was triggered. In addition, she was very detailed, and I could feel myself getting irritated by her questions. I only just survived our first encounter; it was all I could do to hold back and not dismiss her ideas outright. I came away despondent. I did not want to work with her, and I felt the feeling was mutual. I could see disaster ahead because we were in danger of losing an important client.

I spent proper time looking at my own feelings of resentment. I worked through these and eventually got myself to a place where my emotions were no longer loaded – in fact quite the opposite. I began to see her for what she was: a talented young lady with skills beyond mine when it came to taking this project to the next level. I could also see that her requirements plainly did not fit with my skills, and I had to get myself out of the way. I felt a sense of loss but knew I had to let go of this project.

Fortunately, back in the office we had someone who was very good at detail. I assigned her to the programme and introduced her to Maureen. They got on like a house on fire. The project continued and grew positively for another three years. Had I not looked within, I would have hung on to my prejudices, allowed my ego to take charge, and lost one million pounds' worth of business.

Self-empowerment is important to all, but the higher we go up the management chain, the more critical it becomes. At the CEO level, if we are not living in our power, we fail to inspire and lead. Others take over and do as they think fit, and chaos ensues. When we are empowered, those around us know where they fit in, feel recognised and valued, and are enthused to follow our direction.

For Your Consideration

1. At the end of each day, make a note of how empowered you felt during the day. Give yourself a score out of ten for each of the various situations in which you found yourself. Do this for a week and see what revelations emerge.

_____

_____

_____

_____

_____

_____

_____

_____

_____

_____

_____

_____

2. Spend five minutes at the start of every day in a quiet place, and ask yourself what you can change that day to reinforce your feelings of self-empowerment. Consciously drop or delegate all tasks or meetings that you feel have no real meaning; replace them with activities that you know will empower you. Do this also for at least a week.

_____

_____

_____

_____

_____

_____

_____

_____

_____

_____

_____

_____

_____

3. What proportion of your time is spent with clients and on tasks you genuinely enjoy? Once you have estimated this, spend a day or two observing whether it is accurate. How can this proportion be increased by 50 per cent?

_____

_____

_____

_____

_____

_____

_____

_____

_____

_____

_____

_____

_____

_____

_____

CHAPTER 8

The Quantum Leap of Co-Creation and Joint Purpose

What Is Co-Creation?

Co-creation is the joining together of people to produce a mutually valued outcome. In business, it is the cultivation of win-win solutions where efficiency, success, and staff fulfilment march hand in hand. Team members feel respected and honoured, and they know their contributions make a difference. Job satisfaction and creativity Is ignited, there is a positive flow of ideas, and problems get solved in surprisingly simple and practical ways. Staff remain loyal and stay longer because they love what they do.

To be a successful entrepreneur in the twentieth century meant you had to be single-minded, resourceful, and committed. The boss took the responsibility and the risk, and he made the decisions; the employees did as instructed and contributed their time and effort. This has changed. There is large-scale acceptance that staff respond far better when they are genuinely involved. They are eager to contribute and perform beyond expectations when positively encouraged to do so.

For the entrepreneur, co-creation can be a challenge, a real anathema. The building of a business demands resolve and determination to push through ideas in the face of disbelief and scepticism. For those who have honed such skills, co-creation may not come naturally. They struggle to let go of being in charge, and risk blocking further evolution of the business. Maybe this is due to a subconscious belief that no one can do the job as well as them – or indeed, a dread that others may do it better.

The Advantages of Co-Creation

In my experience, it is feasible to run your own business in a completely hands-on manner up to a turnover of £750,000 pa. In our case, this required two of us and a couple of dedicated staff. This level of activity produced a good income, but the business itself lacked intrinsic value. We could never have sold it for a price that would have made us financially independent; it depended too much on us, and any potential buyer would have been quick to point this out. For our company to have explicit value, it needed to grow beyond the four of us and thrive of its own accord. In order to achieve this, we needed to learn how to trust others, truly integrate them, and give them legitimate management responsibilities. We also chose to actively instil a spirit of co-creation. It's more fun to share the load.

Co-creation must be stimulated from the top; if the owners of the business do not want it to happen, it never will. In my own case, I had a head start. Although I am good at coming up with ideas, I know I rarely produce the finished article; I need others to complete the picture. I get a thrill when someone seizes on an idea, takes it on in their own way, and makes a success of it. The test for me is at what stage and in what way to hand over responsibility. If I delegate too quickly, there is no momentum and things collapse. If I hang on too long I restrain others and stifle their creativity.

During the afternoon whilst visiting a trade show, I was beginning to feel weary. I got a nice surprise. The organisers were offering head and shoulder massages – the type of service one sometimes sees at airports. I went for it immediately. It was such a pleasure, and afterwards I felt totally revived for the remainder of the day. What a fabulous service.

Shortly afterwards, we were considering taking a booth at a trade show in Paris. It was our first show, and we wanted to do something different but didn't know what. Inspired by the head and neck massage, I had an idea. We would offer foot massage on our stand, in return for the participants responding to a survey. They were the clinicians from whom medical equipment manufacturers need feedback. It seemed fair to offer massage in exchange for them answering a few questions. I chose foot massage because they would be free to talk. No point in them having their heads down, enjoying a shoulder massage but being unable to speak.

I put the idea to our team. There was a fair degree of laughter and initial hesitation, but we had a general feeling that if we could pull it off, it would be great. We discussed the practicalities, and Sarah, our research operations manager, wanted to make it happen. She expressed one major concern: she did not feel happy about the clinicians having to answer a questionnaire. She preferred that we give the massage without expecting anything in return. Also, she wanted to extend the offer to the other exhibitors – the manufacturers themselves.

I struggled with the idea of not making any money out of our offering. There were costs involved: we had to hire a masseuse and provide space on our stand. I could have insisted that we implement my idea of running a survey, but I resisted. Sarah was in charge, had totally immersed herself in the show, and was bristling with ideas. I decided it was time to let go. We went with her suggestions, and I was delighted we did. The clinicians had come from across the world and were from many different disciplines. It would have been impossible to make meaningful sense of any survey.

The massage attracted huge attention from fellow stand holders, who were over the moon at being able to come by and have their feet revived. Our stand proved to be immensely popular, and many of those who came by turned into potential new customers. Whilst they were having their massage, I was able to introduce myself and present our company. No one refused my offer, and I was able to engage with them in an entirely relaxed atmosphere, where I had their complete attention and gratitude. One key buyer whom we had been pursuing for months returned to the stand every day. She now looks upon us as personal friends and the most creative of all the research companies she has encountered. After having free rein to follow her inspiration, Sarah did a fabulous job, we made lots of new positive contacts, and we had created an outcome better than I could ever have imagined.

With co-creation in place, businesses grow in innovative ways that surpass the imagination of the business owner. We experience the joy of being able to build a business that goes beyond our dreams and simultaneously enables our staff to realise their full potential.

Integrating the Ah But-ers

Many organisations have change averse people who automatically object to new thinking. They are the ones who, just as soon as anything innovative is suggested, come up with a theory as to why it cannot work. Sometimes they initiate doubt behind the scenes or fail to do their part, and they have very valid reasons as to why. Their favourite phrase is, 'Ah, but …'

Such people are a challenge, but when integrated they can turn out to be our best teachers. The way forward starts with active listening. People who resist change are on some level living in fear, and when we make ourselves fully present and listen to them in an open way, without judgement, they feel heard and supported. Their fears dissolve, and they begin to let their barriers down.

One essential tactic is not to argue – in fact, quite the opposite. I ask people to expand on what they are saying until such time as I completely understand them, and I repeat back what I have heard them say. This is called pacing, and it is clear proof that people have been fully heard. The effect can be so freeing and uplifting that they relax their resistance sufficiently to give the new idea a proper try. I have even seen cases where people have completely turned around and become strong advocates for whatever it was they were previously set against. On other occasions, they have talked through their objections to the point where they came up with a solution to their own concerns.

How to Stimulate Co-Creation

Co-creation requires both active listening and intuition. People often express new ideas very tentatively, and it is important not to dismiss them because they appear illogical. This is where intuition comes in. When we sense someone is seeking to explore something, it is crucial to allow space for him to expand on his thoughts. I have noticed someone may say something that appears inconsequential, but the comment strikes a chord in me. Always I go back and ask for a deeper understanding. I never regret doing this, and it often pays dividends.

Co-creation starts by encouraging everyone to speak out, but this can only happen when people feel they trust one another. We actively cultivate trust when we:

- Resist judgement and condemnation. Criticising others is a subtle form of attack, and it causes those on the receiving end to close down or counterattack.
- Are able to live with uncertainty and maintain faith in others when things go wrong. People respond

best when they are allowed to sort out their own messes. We need to indicate we are available to help if required, but if we step in and sort it, we emasculate them. Holding faith that they will find their own answers boosts their confidence.

- Let go of all compulsion to obsessively control. As we allow others to take charge, we see their strengths and abilities, and our confidence in them increases.

- Admit our own vulnerabilities. This is an expression of our trust. It demonstrates our authenticity and opens the door for others to be honest with us.

When co-creation is achieved, there is a genuine buzz that is not hysterical but is definitely palpable. Staff are excited by how their own roles contribute to the overall success of the company, and they have resolve and confidence. People put themselves forward and commit to getting things done. Decisions are taken relatively easily, problems are solved efficiently, and fresh ideas come, even from those more restrained. There is a positive sense of expectation, and new business ideas emerge quite effortlessly.

Co-Creation with Spirit

Co-creation on a human level is highly rewarding both materially and personally. However, there is another form of co-creation that is just as powerful – and on occasion more so – yet is totally undervalued in business. It is co-creation with our Higher Self, or Spirit. This is the essence within each of us, which is all-seeing and remains forever changeless. It knows what is truly in our best interests and what our full potential is. To some this will sound like woo-woo, but in my own life, I have found it works.

In practice, co-creation with Spirit shows up as a step-by-step guide as to what best to do next. Once we had decided to commit ourselves to the niche market of medical devices, we needed a foot in the door. We had one relevant project under our belt, but it was a one-off with a small player. The interesting market was dominated by big, international, blue-chip companies, and somehow we had to make an impact despite being a tiny UK company. Sue started putting together a database of potential clients. My task was to establish contact and introduce our services to the European heads of research and marketing. Such people are very busy and have no time to waste talking to novices. I knew that if and when I did manage to present our company, I would need a very compelling argument for using us rather than the established competition. I definitely needed help.

When we have a strong desire for something that is in alignment with our Higher Selves, the universe makes it available. It may not necessarily be an obvious 'This is what you do now', but more an intuitive hunch that we can heed or not, and it is often repeated in different ways. In my own case, I had been listening to some Tony Robbins recordings entitled *Awaken the Giant Within*. Tony is an impressive motivational speaker, and hearing his words inspired me to go on one of his workshops. During the weekend, we were asked to draft what he referred to as our 'Big Fat Promise'. This had to be the most convincing and powerful statement we could make to a potential client regarding our services or products. It needed to be an absolute stunner, a statement that could not be ignored.

I worked hard on this. Market research is not a subject that grabs people's attention, and so I had to focus on the benefits and push them to their limits. I eventually came up with the following.

> Our company assists medical device manufacturers design products ahead of the competition and develop marketing strategies and campaigns that ensure absolute success. If I could show you how we can help you significantly improve your company's

profitability by bringing to market world beating products, you would be interested, wouldn't you?

Such a statement is of course exaggerated. Market research certainly contributes to good product design and effective marketing, but it does not guarantee success. There are lots of other factors involved, but I needed to seize attention. The alternative was to be ignored. After formulating my promise, I tried it on a couple of others at the workshop. The energy levels were high, people were pushing themselves to their own personal limits, and I was able to practise in a safe environment.

A couple weeks later, I went to my first ever medical device trade show. This was long before we had contemplated having our own stand at such an event, but I knew the exhibitors were our target market. I walked around not engaging with anyone, mentally rehearsing my promise, and getting very nervous. I had been fired up in the workshop, but I was now a nervous wreck; my opening lines sounded stupid, and I feared that as soon as I came out with it, I would become a huge joke. My fear was typical of the moment when we are asked to follow our intuition and do something outside our comfort zone. It is scary, but we simply have to try it.

I walked onto a stand and approached one of the representatives. He politely asked who I was, and after briefly announcing my name, I delivered the promise. To my astonishment, he smiled and said, 'Really? Then you had better meet my colleague over here. He is from marketing.' I was hugely relieved at not being immediately ridiculed, and I delivered the promise a second time. I was asked a couple of superficial questions around which markets we operated in and whether or not I was familiar with the sector. I responded adequately, and to my delight I received the name and contact details of the European marketing director. That person was not available, but I was invited to make contact. I felt things were going my way. I had the name of precisely the right person, and because I had been referred to him, I had a reason to phone once the event was over. The 'Big Fat Promise' proved itself to be exactly what I needed at that time. In one day I was given twenty good names to pursue, and on a few occasions I even managed introductory conversations with precisely the right people.

This was co-creation with Spirit in action. By listening to a Tony Robbins tape, I was inspired to go on a workshop. By attending that, I was given a tool to prise open the door of a number of blue-chip companies and have the occasion to put it to the test. I had yet to win any business, but I knew the names of the individuals I needed to target. I was on my way.

Effortless Accomplishment

There is an underlying belief in Western culture that we need to push ourselves hard in order to achieve success. There is certainly truth in this. It is important to stretch ourselves beyond our comfort zones, break from our ego beliefs, and gain access to new levels of achievement. However, it is counterproductive to push ourselves too hard and for too long. When we do, we introduce fatigue, our focus lapses, things go wrong, and we attract disaster.

Traditional Eastern philosophies such as Zen Buddhism have much to teach us in this area, especially with regard to the concept of effortless accomplishment. The basic principle is that there exists a natural flow of energy through us, and when we are in tune with it, we feel in harmony with all we come into contact with. This is a state of being in co-creation or alignment with Spirit, and we all experience it at times. Our day progresses fluidly, we find ourselves performing tasks at just the right moment, and we achieve substantially more than we had anticipated. This is effortless accomplishment.

Back in the office after my visit to the trade show, I was eager to follow up by phone. I wanted to make contact as quickly as possible and set up face-to-face appointments to present our company and services. I knew that with each call, I had only a few seconds to make an impact; otherwise the person at the other end would hang up or switch off mentally. On each call I enthusiastically reiterated the promise, listened to the responses, did my best to build the conversations, and made face-to-face sales appointments wherever possible. The approach worked well, but I began to notice something. When I was feeling good, I achieved a positive result. The person I was calling was present more often than not and took my call, and we had a useful conversation. On the other hand, the moment I started to feel hesitant, doubtful, or bored, I suffered rejection or bad timing. The person I was after was not interested or not available. The results I achieved were a reflection of how I felt on a minute-by-minute basis.

I was keen to get the calls done. We needed the work, and I feared that as every day passed, the relevance of being able to refer to the trade show diminished. A knee-jerk response would have been to carry on blindly and force myself to keep picking up the phone. On some occasions I did precisely this, but I regretted it. I knew my list was limited, and I did not want to waste it. I started to take regular breaks and check in with myself as to how I was feeling prior to making each call. I eventually established a pattern that worked. I was happy making the calls once a day for ninety minutes. It was considerably less than I had anticipated, but it was highly effective.

Cold calling is an intense experience. The tone of your voice, how well you listen and build your case, and how you instantly respond to new information demands peak alertness. For me, this was a live demonstration of how the world I was experiencing reflected my inner state. When I was feeling focussed and in tune with my natural flow of energy, I achieved good results. If I pushed myself too hard, I blocked the flow and lost connection with my Higher Self, and my efforts backfired.

Overall, I achieved face-to-face sales presentations with seven of the top device manufacturers worldwide. One evolved into a significant client within a couple of months and a few others converted over a longer time frame. I am not saying that the 'Big Fat Promise' will work for everyone, but at that moment in time it was exactly what I needed.

How to Stimulate Co-Creation with Spirit

Co-creation with Spirit is never achieved in our heads alone. It is to be found in a place beyond the egoic mind, where our subconscious and unconscious merge with the universal mind. Such alignment is not easy to attain, but the practice of meditation definitely helps. By shifting our awareness down into our bodies (either into the depth of our bellies or our hearts), closing our eyes, and breathing deeply, we start to calm. A sense of stillness comes to us, and the urgency of time melts away. With continued practice, we begin to experience moments when we sense everything is just as it should be and that we are safe, no matter what is going on in our worlds. It is in this place of centredness and calm that we are guided to what is actually important to get done that day. We live totally in the moment and draw to us that which we need to support us. Our inspiration and intuition are activated, and we move to effortless accomplishment.

Co-creation with Spirit requires constant repetition. Morning meditation gets us off to a good start, but the world we live in throws up challenges all the time. Egoic thinking takes hold again and again, and we feel ourselves getting out of balance, angry, or depressed. At such times it is essential to create space and time to refocus on our breathing, sink mentally back into our bodies, and be as present as possible. A couple of minutes on our own in a quiet place, even the washroom, can be enough.

Joint Purpose

Whilst joint purpose incorporates co-creation it goes beyond it. Joint purpose prevails where intuition is nurtured and honoured, and decisions are taken in alignment with Higher Self. The traditional barrier between owners and staff evolves into a sense of joined endeavour and conflict and stress are minimised. Everyone commits quite naturally to the vision and well-being of the company and takes pride in their own roles. The business blossoms into a stimulating and invigorating place to work and visitors comment spontaneously on the vibrant and caring atmosphere.

A good example of joint purpose for me arose at an annual team awayday. We hired a nice venue, redirected all calls, and did not peek at emails. In order to affirm trust and sincerity, we started with an invaluable exercise. We each considered and wrote out all our personal and work-related goals for the coming one, three, and five years. We initialled and pinned our objectives on a timeline on the wall and then carefully read them. Nothing was judged or criticised; all goals were accepted and respected. By the end, I sensed we had all opened up and fully shared ourselves.

What emerged was a genuine desire to help each other achieve our personal dreams, regardless of what they were. A new house, a long-term relationship, or the success and happiness of a loved one were typical. I felt I understood everyone in a new way, and during the months that followed, I was able to recognise and join with people as their hopes were realised. I knew just how important those goals were to them.

On the business front, various individual goals were revealed. Some wanted to progress to manager level, and others sought to take specific courses to widen their skills. With regards to myself, my goal was to exceed an annual turnover of one million pounds with a healthy margin. This represented a growth of over 30 per cent, and in my mind it would establish us as a significant player in our line of business. My ambition

110

was clearly shared by my fellow directors, especially by my intended successor. He saw it as a chance to prove himself and felt he was being given the opportunity to make his contribution. This was displayed in the office the next day. He posted large sheets of paper on the wall and thereafter marked up each sale as we progressed through the year. We all knew where we were and how much more we needed to reach our goal. The fact we were so aligned allayed any fears around how we would actually cope with the extra workload; we just knew we would. We had a bunch of personal goals and an overall business goal. Enthusiasm was high, and everyone felt totally committed.

This particular awayday demonstrated to me the power of joint purpose. We achieved our objective of one million pounds' turnover in just ten months, and the momentum achieved carried us through the following year to over two million. Just as significant, all our major personal goals were met.

For Your Consideration

1. What aspect of your business life could be entrusted to someone else? This needs to be something important. Who might be excited to take this on? Talk to the person concerned, and if he or she is enthusiastic, consider putting the person in charge.

_____

_____

_____

_____

_____

_____

_____

_____

_____

_____
_____
_____
_____
_____

2. Who is the worst 'ah but-er' in your life? Practise active listening with the person for a week and note down any changes in his or her attitude and how he or she responds to you.

_____
_____
_____
_____
_____
_____
_____
_____
_____
_____
_____
_____
_____

3. At what times in your life have you felt in effortless accomplishment? What was going on at this time? What might have brought it about?

_____
_____
_____
_____
_____
_____

_____

_____

_____

_____

_____

_____

_____

_____

CHAPTER 9

Route to Abundance

An Abundant Life

A life of abundance for many means great wealth evidenced by splendid houses, luxury cars, exotic holidays, and positions of standing. For entrepreneurs, abundance also includes freedom and creativity. We are only happy if we are able to plough our own furrow, build the businesses we want, and be in charge of our own destiny. Perhaps most important, an abundant life includes good health, loving relationships, and the means to help others.

Many entrepreneurs attach such importance to building their business that they devote all their energies to it. Over the years, their health or relationships suffer, and abundance eludes them. Others maintain a more balanced life, enjoy all of the above, and yet still do not experience a sense of lasting abundance. Why is this?

The entrepreneurial journey is different for everyone, but in this chapter I break it down into four key stages and explore how a lasting sense of abundance can be maximised.

- Starting Out
- Building and Initial Success
- Continuous Reinvention
- Letting Go

I Starting Out

Follow Inspiration

The most important element in setting up a new business is sustained enthusiasm. Others detect and admire it, and they feel moved to give support. The universe likewise acknowledges it and assists. Lots of hard work and dedication is required, and remarkable things can happen.

The source of enthusiasm is inspiration. Inspirational ideas arrive suddenly and out of the blue. They possess a dynamic, uplifting quality and are usually a call to action. They come from connection to Spirit, unlock creativity, and are repeated if not immediately understood. They lead us to where we need to be and frequently give us the initial idea, the seed from which we have the opportunity to create abundance. When ignored, regret and remorse eventually ensue.

Our egos want to reject inspiration, and we frequently hear internal voices telling us that our new intentions are stupid or impossible. Such negativity should be strongly resisted. Inspiration must be respected and nurtured without judgement in order to be built into a vision. It's just like a chrysalis transforming into a butterfly: it needs time to take shape.

I never expose new, inspirational thoughts to cynical acquaintances. They focus on any illogicality and are dismissive, and I risk being talked out of my ideas before they have taken form. Instead, I talk new thoughts through with those with whom I feel comfortable. Even then, I sometimes preface the conversation by saying this is a new idea and is as yet incomplete, but I would appreciate sharing it. True leaders know the value of inspiration and are respectful of it.

Use Visualisation to Achieve Goals

Marketing and business plans are valuable because they quantify objectives, oblige us to think through how our goals can be achieved, and help build cohesion and enthusiasm amongst those involved. Their downside is that they are based on linear, left-brain thinking and make no accommodations for the step changes that happen when working co-creatively and in alignment with Spirit. In this sense, they are restrictive and limiting.

On the other hand, the use of visualisation as outlined in chapter 3 adds a new dimension to business planning. I hold my goal as an image that I am aligned with both mentally and emotionally, and I systematically revisit the image every day. This acts like a magnet. By allowing myself to feel and enjoy the sense of excitement and satisfaction I get from having accomplished my goal, my consciousness opens up to it becoming reality. My ego is bypassed, my usual barriers no longer hold the same power, and I programme myself neurologically into a can-do attitude. I remain focused, suffer fewer distractions, and pull into my existence that which I desire.

The manifestation of our goals demands flexibility. We never know the detail of exactly how our dreams will be realised. When I first visualised a million-pound turnover, I also produced a marketing plan as to how I intended to make it happen, with which clients, and over what time frame. To my astonishment, the goal was achieved ahead of time, but how it came about, the clients involved and how we won them bore little resemblance to the plan.

There are occasions when, no matter how well focused we are, we fail to achieve what we desire. Despite our best efforts, our objectives continually elude us. This was certainly my case when I attended two different auctions and made very appropriate bids on an office we wanted to buy. On both occasions, the prize slipped through my fingers at the very last instant. The universe had seemed to conspire against me, but in actuality I was spared significant unnecessary expense and a property that would have become a millstone around my neck.

Such situations call for deep levels of trust. If we lose ourselves in anger and resentment over what we did not get, we never see what is really going on. Our preoccupation with being victims closes our eyes to seeing the better opportunity. Alternatively, if we trust that, having done the best we could, whatever has happened has happened for a reason, then all will eventually become clear. Sometimes this takes a couple of days; at other times it takes a lot longer. It depends on how attached we are to what we thought we wanted.

II Building and Initial Success

Be Guided by Intuition

Our intuition comes from within and nudges us forward to the successful fulfilment of inspiration. It is an inner voice that we all possess, a wise counsellor and is experienced in our body as gut instinct. Sometimes it is a call to look at things differently, at other times it encourages us to take bold steps towards the realisation of our dream. Just like inspiration, it can be scary because it stretches us and takes us beyond our comfort zones. Whatever it suggests may not make logical sense at first, but in the fullness of time it always does. Intuition thrives in free environments and recoils from perfectionism.

We had just sent out an email offer to our database, and out of courtesy a former client in Chicago sent me his best wishes and said if I was ever in town, I should drop in. My first thought was it was a nice idea, but there was nothing to be gained because he now worked in a company that would never require our services. Something felt wrong in my reaction. I was denying myself in some way, and a few days later it dawned on me that my wife and I had a trip planned to California a couple of months later. To include Chicago, spend time with Tim, and have a day visiting the city would be fun. It felt intuitively right to take up his offer, and so we built in a day's vacation and made the necessary arrangements.

The three of us had lunch together. Everything was very pleasant, and as we were walking back to Tim's office, I found myself asking if he was happy in his present position. He declared he was, and we eventually left. I had not consciously considered Tim as an option, but for some time I had had a strong desire to open up the US market. We had sold a handful of one-off projects in North America, but nothing of substance. We were a small UK business, and I could not see how we could ever afford to engage a US agent.

My question must have stuck in Tim's mind. A few weeks later, his company reorganised, and he was given six months garden leave prior to being made redundant. He let me know he was free, and I asked him whether he would consider being our agent in the United States. He had used our services in the past and knew our market very well. Above all, I liked and trusted him. He was delighted to be asked and accepted my offer. The terms of his notice allowed him to work for us, and because he was still being paid by his previous employer, he was happy to accept a low basic salary and commission on sales. Suddenly we had a highly qualified US agent, and I felt huge excitement.

As luck would have it, after a couple of months a European contact within a large US company passed our name to one of his US colleagues. This person was looking for an agency to conduct international research. It was a blue-chip company, a world leader in its field, and Tim and I went to meet them at their headquarters. The meeting went well, the project fitted our skills, and because we were able to show such a quality US presence, we won the job.

Our first major US-based client was on board. We completed the work successfully, follow-up projects ensued, and these days we enjoy an ongoing relationship with multiple buyers on different sites. Later on, Tim was headhunted by another multinational, and we lost him. I am convinced that his presence and contribution at this first critical sales meeting enabled us to win over this major client. We had gained a solid foothold in the United States, and this had come about by me following my intuition. Cold logic would have blocked any contact from taking place.

Intuition is patient. It repeats its message in different guises and at different times. There comes a point, however, when if we continuously ignore it, the negative consequences we invoke physically stop us and make us take stock. If I had listened to my own intuition before experimenting with paragliding in Turkey, I would have avoided a broken ankle and considerable pain and expense. I failed to do so and suffered severe physical restriction as a result.

Never Buy in to External Causes

When faced with a problem, such as a downturn in sales, we might at first be tempted to find fault with external factors such as the economy, a seasonal glitch, clients putting projects on hold, or going bankrupt. Such responses are debilitating because we can do nothing about them. Worse still, if we buy in to such thinking, we justify inactivity. Unexpected events do happen, but the moment we hold external causes responsible, we relinquish control and give away our power to respond. Laying blame on external factors is the ego's way of avoiding stepping up and taking responsibility, and we must resist this easy way out.

I once employed a manager who frequently commented that because we were based where we were, we would never find the staff we needed to expand the business. Our offices were on the outskirts of a provincial town, and in his mind the type of skilled people we needed were not available. He claimed that anyone of any calibre would prefer to commute to London, where salaries were higher and there was lots more going on. I almost bought into his thinking. We had experienced problems finding good staff, and on the surface his argument had logic.

Fortunately, I did not buy in. The moment we became truly aligned in our purpose, exactly the right people arrived – sometimes spontaneously and with no recruitment costs. Despite being in a niche industry, we attracted dynamic young people with totally appropriate skills. They were tired of commuting into London and wanted to settle in the area. Had I bought into the manager's theory, I would have mentally closed down and not been open to drawing in the people we needed.

We always have to be attentive to the opinions of those around us. Negative thinking can creep in almost unnoticed. When one person buys into the fear-based thoughts of another, limiting beliefs start to spread. It takes awareness to see what is going on, clarity of mind to see through it, and resolve to resist it.

View Every Challenge as an Opportunity

When faced with obstacles, we must remind ourselves that the state of our businesses reflects the state of our minds. With each challenge there is every chance it is our own thinking that is contributing to the issue. We have limiting beliefs somewhere within us, and understanding how we contribute to such problems takes considerable awareness. We need to take a long, hard look at what we have or have not been doing, and the starting point is to ask ourselves two key questions.

i) **Is there any way I am contributing to this problem?**

Our ego will always resist this question because it feels threatened and we have to step beyond it. On an outer level, we can talk to the people whom we trust and feel comfortable with. We need to present them with the issue we are facing in as simple, open, and honest a way as possible. We must avoid seeking self-justification and invite honest feedback. This does take courage – we are admitting our own vulnerability and asking for help. If friends are not on hand, entire strangers can be of benefit. It's surprising how insightful the person sitting next to you on an airplane can be once you get talking.

Friends and others in whom we do confide are unlikely to give us the complete answer. They speak from their own life experiences, but they often provide excellent clues. On an inner level, I find the most important thing to do is to sit quietly and ask myself, 'With regard to … is there any way in which I am contributing to the problem?'

This is an act of humility and an expression of willingness to hear the truth. Whatever comes up may provoke further queries. As I formulate these queries, in order to avoid confusion, it is important to ask clear follow-up questions where a definite yes or no can be given. Provided my intention is correct, I receive the insight I need to take the situation forward, and the responses feel fresh, vibrant, and life enhancing.

After I met Maureen and realised I would be dealing with her rather than Steve, the European marketing director of a major diagnostics company, I knew I was uncomfortable, and our biggest contract was at risk. I sat quietly and took time to ask whether I was contributing to the problem. I received a very definite yes, and began to realise that however I changed my way of communicating with her, I would only be tampering. I then asked whether I should completely remove myself; a clear yes again emerged. I started to ask who I should delegate the project to and just one person popped up. I was a little nervous to start with because I feared this person would not be able to get on with Maureen either. This turned out to be my projection. They got on exceptionally well, the contract not only continued but expanded and I was hardly ever directly involved.

ii) What do I need to learn from this situation?

Working harder and doing more of the same is never the answer to a business situation where we are getting nowhere. There are no challenges that do not potentially bring new wisdom and growth. Complete disasters only occur when we close down and block the new learning that the 'problem' is asking us to embrace. Once again, the approach is to recognise that we are stuck and to consciously sit quietly and ask, 'With regard to ... what do I need to learn from this situation?' It is by asking ourselves honestly and sincerely just what it is we need to learn, that we shift the way we see things and move forward.

III Continuous Reinvention

Invisible Glass Ceilings

There are occasions when we subconsciously elect to stay with our egoic beliefs, and we cannot get beyond them. Self-enquiry does not quite do the job. Maybe we are extremely triggered and have lost ourselves in jealousy, anger, or hurt; we cannot bring ourselves to sit quietly and consider what is really going on. Personally, I have been in this place many times. It is as though I have come up against an invisible glass ceiling, and my self-limiting beliefs are restricting me. Some sort of personal emotional block, an internal demon, has me in its grip, and I either cannot or do not want to face it. I am terrified others will see my incompetence or stupidity. They might even get a glimpse of just how bad I sometimes judge myself to be.

At times like this, we believe we are far from abundance. Despite whatever good things we have going on in our lives, no matter what material wealth we have accumulated, all our thoughts are overwhelmed by whatever is triggering us. We may recognise something is not right, but we feel paralyzed and incapable of tackling it. We also believe that if we expose our fears and true feelings, it will be the end of us. We consider it a sign of weakness to seek help, but help is exactly what we need.

Fortunately for us, we do not get let off the hook. Whatever the difficulty is, it keeps returning in one form or another, constantly urging us to take notice. Continued resistance brings about negative outcomes, and the stakes escalate to the degree that we risk bringing about illness or accident to ourselves. Alternatively, we may suffer the loss of a major contract or similar catastrophe.

Just as we need to constantly reinvent our products or services to stay aligned with changing market needs, we need to continuously reinvent ourselves. By seeking help, we start to grow into our full potential. It takes courage, but by having the humility to accept that we need support, we learn to accept and forgive both ourselves and others. We gain new insight and a deeper understanding of who we really are. We unblock a flow of energy, which has been stifled for years, and move from a place of fear to renewed enthusiasm and empowerment.

I have used the 'Clearing Process' as described in chapter 4, 'Transforming Self-limiting Beliefs', to great effect in order to unravel and clear emotional blocks. The time I hired a new sales manager and discovered after six months that, despite being very busy, he was making no sales, I was hesitant about what to do. He had a confident manner, and given the way he spoke, success was always just around the corner. As each of his 'dead cert' sales fizzled out, he produced perfectly logical reasons as to why – and the excuses never involved him. I knew he could do the job because he had performed well in his first six months, but everything seemed to have come to a halt, and

I had no idea why. I started to question him and put him on the spot, and he became belligerent. Bad feelings crept in, and it became a war of attrition. No one was going anywhere, and the business was suffering as a result.

It took several sessions of egoic clearing for me to release my anger and see that the problem I was experiencing was of my own making. I had given him the job that I wanted. Winning new clients was my own passion, but I had been so engrossed and attached to thinking that I had to attend to existing clients, that I had not seen this. The 'Clearing Process' helped me build up the trust I needed to delegate the responsibility of existing clients to others. I was able to let my sales manager go with minimum upset, and I awarded myself the job I really wanted. From that moment, the business turned around, sales came in, and we once again started to thrive.

Help is always available when we open ourselves up to it. There are many types of advisers, consultants, and counsellors available. When you decide you need one, it is important to choose one you feel you can trust. As a student of *A Course in Miracles*, I favour spiritually based counsellors who work from its principles. I have already mentioned the 'Clearing Process' as offered by Sandy Levey-Lunden and Len Satov, and further details can be seen at www.sandylevey.com. Sarah Alexander is another excellent example, and details of her services can be found at www.sarah-alexander.co.uk. The objective is invariably the same: the alchemical transformation of emotional blocks into new beginnings, restored enthusiasm, and vitality.

For those who are committed to doing their own inner work, the following is a three-step egoic clearing process based on the Course that I recommend.

Step 1: When feeling triggered, I spend time alone getting deeply in touch with the emotion that is coming up within me. I give full vent to it. This is where my energy is, and I must connect with it in order to move forward. I write a completely honest letter to the person concerned, but I do not post it. Sometimes I pretend the person is a cushion and bash the hell out of it. The key is that I get everything said and fully expressed. There then comes a moment when I sense I have said all I need.

It is important not to stop at this stage. Even though there may be a sense of relief at getting everything off my chest, the process is not complete. I need to continue and heal whatever misconceptions I am suffering.

Step 2: I release my feelings by vigorously throwing them up in the air. I hand them over to Spirit with the following words.

I place these feelings/issues about … in the hands of Spirit. I ask that all misconceptions be purified and healed, that I be released from them totally, and that whatever is in the greatest good be manifest for all.

I repeat this several times. A sense of calm comes over me, and a new way of seeing the situation or relationship emerges.

Step 3: I consciously choose to acknowledge and affirm the innocence of the person with whom I was at odds, by saying the following words.

If I see you … as the cause of the problem, then my imagined fear and guilt must be in me. Because we are not separate, I forgive us both for what we thought we did. We are both innocent. I release both you and myself to live our lives to the full and in perfect peace.

This final step is based on the law of forgiveness, as described by Gary Renard in his book *The Disappearance of the Universe.*

Life is unpredictable, and there will always be times when we are knocked back and triggered. The issue is how long we choose to remain in this disempowered state, and how to get out of it. As we practise egoic clearing, we get better at it. It is like a muscle that becomes stronger and more powerful with exercise. The ego will always resist, but as we become increasingly skilful at egoic clearing, it loses its hold over us, and we put our real selves back in the driving seat.

Egoic clearing minimises the time we feel thrown off track by problems. We no longer disengage from abundance and focus on lack. We flex our new muscles and deal proactively with evolving relationships and circumstances. Above all, we reconnect with abundance.

IV Letting Go

When you have spent years building a business, nurturing it, and being totally committed to every aspect of its existence, it is a complete wrench to let it go – but let it go you must. It needs to grow beyond you, and you need to grow beyond it. You have had the fun of creating it, the satisfaction of seeing it blossom and mature, and you've enjoyed all the places and people you would never have otherwise encountered.

Entrepreneurs who are capable of letting go liberate their time and energy to create further businesses, if this is their desire. Alternatively, they enjoy the fruits of their labour and explore different aspects of their creativity. Some become philanthropists and drive significant projects for the good of humanity. Others provide the wherewithal for young entrepreneurs to start up their own companies. In sharp contrast, carrying on running a business when one's passion for it has waned, or one's time with it has passed, is foolish and wasteful. The energy is no longer attuned to the business, and it is far better to move on and see what life has in store next.

Selling a business and letting it go is the opposite of building it. The emotional journey and required mindset are poles apart. To build a business takes big dreams, massive commitment, courage, an eye for a good deal, and discipline to watch and control everything. Letting go pivots on being able to accept that others can do just as good a job – and hopefully, an even better one. We extract ourselves from being at the centre of everything. We are happy to give advice if asked, but otherwise we encourage others to make their own decisions.

Letting go is essentially an act of surrender, but not in the sense of giving in. To surrender in a spiritual sense is to trust so much in our Higher Self that we are prepared to follow its guidance, wherever it takes us and with no attachment to the outcome. This type of surrender does not come from a place of weakness but of absolute trust. If we disagree with someone, we might choose to express our views, but we do not get triggered if our advice is not taken. We have faith that the best solution will always emerge.

Knowing when to let go is difficult. In my own case, I was completely identified with my business and could never have imagined myself doing anything different. I suspect I was fearful that without it, my life would be meaningless, but I was far too absorbed to realise it.

Fortunately, we are always given hints as to when it is time for change. It's our decision whether or not we acknowledge it, but when we do, the process can proceed relatively smoothly. If we resist, we encounter resistance and may be forced to let go in circumstances that we would not have otherwise chosen. In my own case, it was only once I had broken an ankle and was obliged to stay at home that I began to see it was time for change. I realised I wanted to write this book and had the opportunity to start it.

My own process of letting go was much facilitated by having someone in place whom we wanted to move up to

CEO. I had always favoured the idea of an MBO, but that depended upon having the right person to take over the reins. The thought of getting on with the book gave me something to go forward to, as opposed to looking over my shoulder at what I was leaving behind. Without this, I suspect I would have found the whole process much more difficult.

We engaged specialist MBO advisers, and despite the process taking over a year, they earned their fees. There were lots of issues to be thought through, and it paid dividends to have people with practical experience to take us through the process and act as honest broker.

In Conclusion

The experience of having created, built, struggled, survived, prospered, and eventually sold one's own business yields a deep satisfaction that can never be taken away. Significant wealth gives us the freedom to do whatever we want for ourselves and others, and it is both hugely rewarding and liberating. Close friends, positive family ties, and good health are equally as important – no amount of wealth can replace them.

It remains possible to have all of the above but still not feel lasting abundance. The reason is that the ego will always try to get in our way. No matter how much we achieve in life, our ego will always endeavour to find lack somewhere and trick us into believing we are a victim, are guilty, or are unworthy.

Lasting abundance depends on our ability to remain in connection with our Higher Self, our Spirit. Once we develop the awareness to identify when our ego is active, and we perfect our skills in dealing with it, then we remain in connection with the life force. The more we work on our inner beings, the more we free ourselves of fear, consciously step up, reveal the best of ourselves, and inspire others to do likewise. We take proactive action and trust that whatever the outcome, it is ultimately in our best interests. We live in the world but are no longer dependent on it; neither are we influenced by what others think of us. We have deeply rooted trust in the universe, are happy to surrender to it, and genuinely enjoy peace of mind. We are so closely aligned with our Higher Selves and Spirit that the ego no longer holds or affects us.

For Your Consideration

1. What does abundance mean to you?

_____

_____

_____

_____

_____

_____

_____

_____

_____

_____

_____

_____

_____

2. At what stage are you in your business?
   - Starting Out
   - Building and Initial Success
   - Continuous Reinvention
   - Letting Go

_____

_____

_____

_____

_____

_____

_____

_____

_____

_____

_____

_____

_____

_____

3. What is the most significant problem in your business right now? In what way are you contributing to it? What lesson is the problem trying to teach you?

_____

_____

_____

_____

_____

_____

_____

_____

_____

_____

_____

_____

_____

_____

CHAPTER 10

The Visionary CEO

Time for Change

Attitudes to business desperately need to change. Dog-eat-dog mentalities at work lead to mistrust, deceit, and betrayal. Corruption within our banks seems ineradicable, and regulation alone will never curb it. The ruthless pursuit of maximum profit regardless of consequences is ruining the planet and belittles us as an advanced society.

On an individual level, ever increasing levels of stress are causing huge damage to our physical bodies. The emphasis attached to material success is so strong that many of those without it judge themselves a failure and fall prey to depression. High blood pressure, diabetes, obesity, and cancer are reaching epidemic levels and are being diagnosed at younger and younger ages. Whilst our total wealth increases, our general happiness lags behind.

The Visionary CEO

The positive news is that after having reached such extremes, we have an increasing number of visionary CEOs who are committed to change. They know that control and domination no longer work, and are creating open and trusting work environments where people no longer react out of fear. They empower their employees by creating a culture of co-creation: they define clear objectives, provide the necessary resources, trust them to make their own decisions, and get out of the way. Their staff focus on results; a strong sense of openness and community prevails, and innovation is naturally forthcoming. Employee turnover drops, clients love the genuine dedication they receive, market change is identified and responded to ahead of competition, and the company flourishes.

Such visionary CEOs include Sir Richard Branson; his flexible working policy and the resultant benefits in productivity and creativity have already been referred to. Larry Page and Sergey Brin at Google also fit this profile. They discovered that technological breakthrough is enhanced by letting their staff spend 20 per cent of their time on whatever projects they feel passionate about.

Such world-famous entrepreneurs are perhaps held in so much awe that the average sole trader with a few staff finds it difficult to relate to them. They have all the resources to experiment in whatever ways they want, quality people queuing up to work for them, and no weekly battle to pay the bills. However, less well-known visionary CEOs of more national or local renown do exist, and they are mushrooming in numbers. Examples include the following.

i.   Luis Falcao is the South African country manager for BASF Crop Protection. They offer a premium brand of conscientious farming solutions with a non-GMO seal. He views whatever challenges that occur as first and foremost a reflection of what is going on in him. Since his arrival three years ago, he has tripled their turnover and simultaneously increased gross profit. He seeks to make his decisions in alignment with his Higher Self, and he views sustainable financial success as one of the rewards. 'If a leader truly cares about the people he leads, the community and the company he works for, he will do what's fair, just and right. When you offer trust, compassion, hope, stability and security to others, the reward is sustainable success that in turn offers you exactly what you have given.'

ii.   Lauri Feinsod is the CEO of Graphik Dimensions Ltd, a world-leading printing and framing company. She introduced what she calls a 'living the question' mind-set to the business. Everyone is encouraged to question everything, speak openly, and create differently. When she joined the company, she invited interested employees to define their own set of company values, the very highest qualities they aspired to in their work. They came up with C4: consciousness, collaboration, creativity, and community. There is no notice board with grand words gathering dust in reception at GD. The workers understand what is at the heart of the company and drives it forward, because they defined it. All decisions are made and monitored against these values. As a result, GD has achieved consistent growth over the last six years – including doubling the company's top line – and has won ten different awards for its evolutionary culture, sustainable innovations, and explosive growth, including 'Fastest Growing', 'Top Women-Owned', 'Manufacturer of the Year', and 'Best Place to Work'.

iii. Richard Reed of Innocent Smoothies. He actively encouraged his staff to express their personal values and apply them by making socially aware decisions. He awakened their creativity and was supportive if they felt drawn to setting up their own businesses. During a fifteen-year period, he and his team built up a company from scratch to one that sold two million smoothies per week and was sold in recent years for over £300m.

Such CEOs see themselves as connected and interdependent with others. They are at the cutting edge of empowering those who work for them, and they encourage the members of their team to pursue their own goals alongside those of the business. They fund training programmes for young entrepreneurs, sponsor aid programmes in developing countries, and even set up foundations to create positive change in both business and society. They are living examples of how open communication, integrity, and a culture of co-creation bring out the best in everyone.

The Next Wave of Visionary CEO

Change is inevitable and constant. The principles of empowerment, co-creation, and trust have now been proved by sufficient numbers of leading companies that the trend will never be reversed. So what will the next wave visionary CEO look like?

In my opinion, the next evolution will incorporate a belief in Higher Self and a resolve to make decisions in alignment with it. Such CEOs will acknowledge that behind the physical world, there is something of deeper significance, a vision wanting to be revealed. It is this that will add new meaning to the term 'visionary CEO', and each entrepreneur's realisation of it will be an important contribution to the well-being of all. Some of those mentioned may even already embody this but refer to it in some other way, or they simply prefer to keep it private. Luis Falcao is certainly quite open about his spiritual beliefs.

Until I was able to connect with my own Higher Self, I reacted according to my limited egoic interpretation of whatever was going on around me. I failed to pursue what I intuitively knew to be right, and sometimes I self-sabotaged. I judged others too readily and did not draw the best from them.

I lacked the bedrock upon which I could make consistently good decisions. Once I acknowledged my own Higher Self, I began to see the real opportunities behind what was presented to me. I started to recognise when I was being obsessive about being right, and I questioned my own motives. I consciously nurtured, trusted, and followed my intuition.

From this moment, my wife, Sue, and I committed to the process of egoic clearing, and as a result we started to see others in their Truth. We were effectively relating to the Higher Selves in others, and we evoked the best from them. When challenges came up, we asked ourselves where we might be contributing to the problem and what we needed to learn from the situation. We corrected mistakes without judging others or ourselves, moved on, and left no sense of bitterness behind. We attracted staff in alignment with our values. In turn, they brought their own gifts, and the business was always enhanced as a result. It was not an easy journey – we suffered many setbacks, and I often felt I was trying to pull myself up by my own shoe laces. Eventually, however, the vagaries of life as a harassed sole trader started to fade into the past.

To the outer world, we were an up-and-coming market research company, In fact, we were one of the fastest growing in Europe, and at over 20 per cent net profit, we were one of the most profitable. In terms of the bigger picture, our vision was realised. We were a deeply bonded team that was united through compassion for and understanding of one another, including those with whom we did business. We genuinely cared for and supported one another. Everyone enjoyed coming to work and gave their absolute best. Above all, I was profoundly happy that I had grown as a person and been able to integrate and live out my spirituality in business.

Balancing Spirituality with Practicality

Many hard-nosed business people will flinch at the idea of seeking first and foremost to trust others, and they will readily cite examples of untrustworthy characters who have tried to cheat them. The concept of trust in a Higher Self can even provoke greater disdain, and to a degree this scepticism is justified. Much spiritual teaching is viewed as utopian, airy fairy, and not applicable in the tough world of business. The skill of the next wave of visionary CEOs will lie in the ability to balance metaphysical principles with savvy and common sense; naivety serves no one. Such is the case when entering into significant business deals. Trust is the glue that unites people, and it is highly rewarding to see it pay off, but the right structures need to be in place to support everyone should things go wrong.

The basis of our own MBO involved a huge level of trust. The majority of our settlement was left outstanding in the business, and once we stepped away, our financial future depended on its success over a five-year period. If the company failed, we risked being left with comparatively little financial reward. Also, our purchaser was relatively young, and although he already owned a small percentage of the business, he was not putting any personal cash into the deal; he was not in a position in his life where he could. Our lawyers believed we were crazy to expose ourselves in this way, and although we acknowledged their opinions, we instructed them to continue.

We never regretted our decision, but we did spend many hours going over the eventualities of what would happen if the business got into difficulty and payments were not forthcoming. The process demanded absolute openness and honesty, and experienced advisers were essential. By the end, we felt that if things did not work out, at least we knew where we stood. I have known other entrepreneurs who have come out of businesses feeling deceived and betrayed, and I wanted to ensure I had done the maximum to avert inappropriate expectations and misunderstanding.

It is difficult to define when to rely on trust alone and when to include more formal structures to cater for the unexpected. One thing for sure is that it is far better to trust and sometimes be disappointed, than to be forever mistrusting and live in fear. The visionary CEO is primarily grounded in trust; he or she weighs up the facts and relies on intuition and inner guidance when making decisions. Energy is not wasted considering negative what-if scenarios, but attention is paid to warning signals and any feedback indicating that something needs attention. He or she trusts that if a wrong decision has been made, it will be flagged in some form or another and can be dealt with at that time.

The Time Scale of Higher Intelligence

On how many occasions in your life have you noticed that things took longer than anticipated but worked out far better than you expected? The visionary CEO has the courage to surrender to the time scale of higher intelligence. He or she stays in the present and opens up to whatever it was that was not planned, in the knowledge that it will be better than what was.

When we first envisaged our MBO, we engaged a specialist lawyer and a corporate tax adviser – only to fire them after five months. We really did not like where they were taking us and pulled out rather than sign a deal that none of us liked or fully understood. It was a brave move. We had an agreed deadline, the new CEO wanted to get started, and the temptation was to complete. We had already invested lots of time and money, and it would have been easy to assume the professionals knew best and sign the contracts. We did not. We followed our intuition and, after a break, started all over again with new advisers.

Overall, the deal took an additional eighteen months, but we fully understood what we were doing and were happy about it. Also, during this time the business was going through a tremendous period of growth, and the additional eighteen months allowed the benefit of this to be reflected in its value. Had we done the deal as originally scheduled, we would have received 30 per cent less than we did.

Adieu to the Harassed Sole Trader

I was over sixty by the time I learned how to express my spiritual beliefs in my business and had it generating consistently healthy profits independent of me. Others will achieve this in much shorter time frames. The end result is important, but the actual journey is equally as rewarding and significant. Three steps forward will be followed by one step back, but the backward step will provide just the right insight to be able to step up to something far better.

Bidding adieu to the harassed sole trader and transitioning to this new form of visionary CEO will demand an openness to look within, a willingness to let go of old patterns of thinking, and a determination to change. If prolonged periods of time are spent in what feels like the doldrums, there is probably something not right, and significant change in mindset is required.

This book is primarily written for the sole trader who has been in business for some time, is struggling to achieve consistent success, oscillates between good and bad years, and battles to find and keep the right staff. If you are such an entrepreneur and want to bid adieu to such a life in order to experience the results and abundance you deserve, then I recommend four key regular practices.

1. Discipline of the Mind

Daily meditation ensures that you start the day on the right foot. It helps you avoid getting side-tracked by all the needless issues to which the egoic mind would prefer you devote your attention.

Staying in the present during the day is challenging. For myself, I use the daily themes of the workbook in *A Course in Miracles*. If you do not feel drawn to this, you might find the practice of mindfulness helpful. I would suggest reading *Mindfulness for Dummies* by Shamash Alidina.

2. Ongoing Egoic Clearing

Life constantly throws up new challenges. Living authentically involves rising above the crowd and being different. It means giving up smallness and letting go of the need for approval from others. The practice of egoic clearing frees you from fear and moves you to a new level of awareness. You change, see new options, and move on.

As your consciousness evolves and you become established in new ways of thinking, your egoic mind will present you with new challenges. This is grist to the mill, and the new material, when transformed, lifts you again to another level. Without it, you risk settling with the status quo and slipping into predictability. Instead, you turn again to egoic clearing and work on whatever the new obstacle is presenting to you.

The key is to find and work with a spiritually aligned coach whom you trust and feel intuitively drawn to. This person must challenge you, albeit in a positive and constructive way. Also, as your situation evolves, be prepared to change the method of clearing – and if appropriate, the coach too. There are different techniques available, and some suit particular people or situations more than others. In all cases, the benefits must remain observable.

3. Use of Intuition and Alignment with Spirit

Seek to cultivate and follow your intuition; it is your guide and will protect you. Experiment and establish what it is that nurtures it and build this into your schedule. Make friends with your intuition and follow it boldly.

Consciously align with Spirit through meditation or prayer. Ask for guidance using clear questions and avoid getting caught out by your ego. Accept that when things do not work out the universe holds something better. See and relate to everyone as their true selves ie their Higher Selves, and do not get sucked into their egoic thinking, however badly they are behaving. You will continue to face challenges and sometimes make mistakes, but you will learn from your errors quickly, grow personally, and become more trusting.

When we are fully congruent with Spirit, we gain a quietness of mind and the ability to receive guidance at all times. Eventually you arrive at a real sense of abundance, far in excess of any personal wealth.

4. Live Beyond Your Comfort Zone

When you follow your intuition, seek guidance, discipline the mind, and commit to ongoing egoic clearing, you will be constantly nudged out of your comfort zone. The more you practise and get comfortable with this, the more confidence you will gain. You will continue to make mistakes, but there will be fewer of them, and you will rectify them quickly.

I am grateful for all the obstacles I experienced on my own journey. Every sleepless night was worth it. Without all the challenges, I would never have learned what I needed to learn. The outcomes always exceeded whatever I had initially envisaged. There were no losers; our success was never at the expense of anyone else. We created no enemies, left no skeletons in the cupboard, and departed the business in excellent physical health.

The new wave of visionary CEOs will desire personal wealth and will wholeheartedly enjoy it. They will regard money as a tool, a form of energy that needs to be in flow, put to good use, and not jealously hoarded. They will ask themselves how they can best serve others and the greater good, both within their businesses and outside them, and they will actively seek to ensure that their companies enhance the lives of those they touch.

Alignment with Spirit will become a primary goal. Compassion will oust conflict, and trust, integrity, and joint purpose will become the norm rather than the exception. These CEOs will take the culture of business to an entirely new level, encompassing new standards of which we are all proud. They will inspire others in business to come out with their own spiritual beliefs and reveal the truth of who they really are. A halt will be drawn to all sorts of greed, malpractice, and dishonesty. Entrepreneurship will be regarded as a noble profession that contributes to the good of humanity, not just the few. A sense of abundance will prevail, and the world will be a far better place for it.

For Your Consideration

1. On a scale of one to five, where one represents the harassed sole trader and five is the visionary CEO, where would you position yourself and why?

_____

_____

_____

_____

_____

_____

_____

_____

_____

_____

_____

_____

_____

_____

2. In what ways could you show up as your real authentic self and express your highest ideals?

_____

_____

_____

_____

_____

_____

_____

_____

_____

_____

_____

3. What are you prepared to commit to in order to ensure you realise the visionary CEO within yourself?

_____

_____

_____

_____

_____

_____

_____

_____

_____

_____

_____

_____

BIBLIOGRAPHY

Chapter 2: Power of Intuition

Peirce, Penney. *The Intuitive Way*. New York: Atria Books, 2009.

Williams, Nick. *The Work You Were Born to Do*. India: Balloon View: 2010.

Chapter 3: Vision Outperforms Planning

Kehoe, John. *Mind Power into the 21st Century*. Vancouver: Zoetic Inc: 2011

Dispenza, Joe. *Evolve Your Brain: Breaking the Habit of Being Yourself*. Florida: Health Communications Inc: 2007

Tolle, Eckhart. *Stillness Speaks*. Vancouver: Namaste Publishing: 2003

Hicks, Esther and Jerry. *Ask and It Is Given*. Carlsbad, California: Hay House: 2004

Chapter 5: Integrity and Trust Are Gold Standards

Richo, David. *Daring to Trust.* Boston and London: Shambhala Publications: 2010

Richard Branson. www.virgin.com/richard-branson.

Chapter 6: Forgiveness Leads to Freedom

Ford, Debbie. *Dark Side of the Light Chasers.* London: Hodder and Stoughton: 2001

The Foundation for Inner Peace. *A Course in Miracles.* Mill Valley, California: Foundation for Inner Peace: 2007

Chapter 8: The Quantum Leap of Co-Creation and Joint Purpose

Robbins, Tony. *Awaken the Giant Within* (audiobook). London: Simon and Schuster Audio: 2005

Chapter 9: The Route to Abundance

Levey-Lunden, Sandy. The Clearing Process. www.sandylevey.com and www.lensatov.com

Alexander, Sarah. www.sarah-alexander.co.uk

Renard, Gary. *The Disappearance of the Universe.* Carlsbad, California: Hay House: 2004

Chapter 10: The Visionary CEO

The Evening Standard. We want to pass on that business karma. Feature on Richard Reed, Innocent Smoothies. 14 February, 2014

Alidina, Shamash. *Mindfulness for Dummies*. Chichester, England: John Wiley & Sons: 2013

GLOSSARY

Higher or Spiritual Self: The essence within us that is eternally connected to Spirit. It is forever changeless, is all-knowing, and remains at peace no matter what is going on in our lives.

We experience our Spiritual Selves when we feel at one with everything and everyone around us, and we have a sense of calm beyond all forms of stress. We recognise that all that has ever happened makes sense and has purpose, and we know that whatever the future brings, it will be exactly what is required. We fully comprehend that we are forever safe.

Higher Guidance: The voice of our Spiritual Selves

Spirit: The essence within each of us which connects us to all of life. It is an all-powerful energy and pure love.

Inspiration: A big idea that seems to arrive spontaneously out of the blue. It has a dynamic, uplifting quality and is a call to action. It comes to us from Higher Guidance and unlocks creativity, and the message is usually repeated if not immediately understood. It leads us to where we need to be and frequently gives us the initial idea, the seed from which we have the opportunity to create abundance. When completely ignored, regret and remorse ensue.

Intuition: Comes from within and tends to nudge us forward in our lives. It is experienced in our body as gut instinct, and it is a call to question what is going on and to look at things differently. It is an inner voice that we all possess and a wise counsellor. It also comes from Higher Guidance, is repeated in various forms, thrives in free environments, and abhors perfectionism. Just like inspiration, it can be scary, especially at first, because it stretches us and takes us beyond our comfort zone. Step by step, however, our intuition guides us to the successful fulfilment of inspired ideas, and in the fullness of time it makes complete sense. When ignored, we can experience increasing degrees of discomfort until such time as we take heed.

Printed in the United States
By Bookmasters